GETTING Real ABOUT GETTING OLDER

Conversations about Aging Better

Linda K. Stroh, PhD
Karen K. Brees, PhD

sourcebooks

Published by Sourcebooks, Inc.
P.O. Box 4410, Naperville, Illinois 60567-4410
(630) 961-3900
Fax: (630) 961-2168
sourcebooks.com

Library of Congress Cataloging-in-Publication Data

Names: Stroh, Linda K., author. | Brees, Karen K., author.
Title: Getting real about getting older : conversations about aging better / Linda K. Stroh, PhD, and Karen K. Brees, PhD.
Description: Naperville, Illinois : Sourcebooks, [2018] | Includes bibliographical references and index.
Identifiers: LCCN 2018010650 | (pbk. : alk. paper)
Subjects: LCSH: Aging. | Aging--Psychological aspects. | Aging--Physiological aspects.
Classification: LCC QP86 .S755 2018 | DDC 612.6/7--dc23 LC record available at https://lccn.loc.gov/2018010650

Printed and bound in the United States of America.
VP 10 9 8 7 6 5 4 3 2 1

To my family—Greg, Angie, Joe, Brad, Brandy, Brayden,
and Brooke—who make life meaningful in indescribable ways,
and to my treasured friends throughout my life who have helped
me grow older, better.
—Linda

To Harmon and Ann—ninety-three years old
and the youngest in spirit.
—Karen

Table of Contents

WHAT'S THIS AGING THING ALL ABOUT?

O ld people don't wear jeans. Old people don't listen to rock music. And old people certainly don't put selfies on Facebook. Those may be commonly held beliefs among young people about their parents and grandparents, but of course, older people do all of these things.

While we may love our iPhones, iPads, and selfies as much as the younger generation, our bodies and minds are changing. Although we may not want to admit it, it's true: we're getting old. In fact, we are old! As this book goes to press, Linda is seventy, and Karen is nearly seventy-two. There's no denying it—we are officially *old*. That realization was the impetus for our writing this book.

We can't figure out how it happened, and we can't believe we were so unprepared for it, but here we are. And, after some reflection, we've concluded that getting old doesn't have to be something we dread or worry about—it's not a bad thing. In fact, we believe our older years can be the very best ones of our lives. After reading this book, we hope you will agree.

Getting Real about Getting Older is neither a research study nor an academic undertaking. We are not attempting to argue a point or contribute to the already extensive academic literature on the topic of aging. Rather, our interest over the course of three years of conversations with people aged sixty-five and older was in discussing the physical and psychological experiences of aging with as many people as we could. We reached nearly one thousand participants eager to discuss their feelings about growing older. What we found special and unique about our conversations with our diverse group of aging respondents was how willing they were to share their deepest and most gut-wrenching experiences, along with their insights into the happier aspects of aging.

We soon realized that few of our respondents had ever been asked their thoughts about growing older, and for many, this was the first time they had thought seriously about the topic. They were eager to answer questions, ask questions, offer advice, and help us in our quest to discover how to grow older, *better*.

We developed a broad-spectrum questionnaire that invited respondents to share their ideas on a variety of topics— from relationships with spouses, partners, and their adult children, to the role of a belief system in their lives. We asked about love, loss, changing identities, and any lessons learned along the way. We invited our respondents to speak about their problems with their adult children, as well as the joys of grandparenting and great-grandparenting. We asked them to respond to our suggested topics or speak whatever was on their minds. The topics they chose were ones that people struggle with throughout their lives—relationships, loss, family, health, sex. We discovered that every issue we face as younger people takes on a different hue as we age.

Our respondents repeatedly told us that only adolescence had been as physically and emotionally challenging as this time of life, and they were unprepared for the dramatic physical, psychological, and emotional changes taking place in their later years. That was an important point, and it reinforced our belief that we had, with this book, the chance to change lives by providing comfort, information, and, in a very real sense, friendship for readers experiencing the challenges and joys of aging.

We began by chatting with a wide spectrum of people sixty-five and older, asking what issues were most important to them during these later years of their lives. We emailed our survey to everyone we knew; handed it out to friends, family, and neighbors; and posted it on every Listserv we belonged to—and a few we didn't. We contacted relevant community and book groups—if older people were there, we were too, ready to talk about aging. We struck up conversations at the airport, in line at the grocery store, in the waiting rooms at doctor's offices, at the Laundromat—wherever we happened to be. We spoke with people we knew and with total strangers. Over coffee, with groups of friends, we discussed the issues common to all of us sixty-five and older. We read magazine articles and consulted the academic literature about aging, looking for examples to give clarity and support to each "Reality Check," the helpful tips we include in each chapter for dealing with aging-related issues. And we looked at government statistics on various health and longevity topics to explore common points of anxiety.

Throughout our book, we've included excerpts from conversations with our many respondents. In some cases, we edited for clarity and paraphrased content taken from group discussions and interviews. Many of our respondents shared similar stories, and we combined the highlights from these stories to create a narrative of these common experiences. We mainly focused on problems we may encounter as we age, although we do take some time to also highlight the more positive aging experiences we all have enjoyed. To guarantee our respondents' anonymity, we omitted names from our quotes and replaced them with sometimes humorous, other times unusual, descriptors. We had an inherent advantage in initiating conversations with our respondents—we were part of the group we were seeking to understand. Relating to older people came naturally to us. We simply wanted to know what people were thinking—what their concerns and experiences were with getting older. Our goal was to provide a snapshot of their lives. We wanted our readers to know they were not on this journey alone, that many others shared their concerns about aging and many had similar stories to tell. Where concerns were raised by some, others provided responses and advice. As a result, our book is essentially a series of shared conversations that revealed to us the heartbeat and the soul of older America.

The interest we received in our project was phenomenal. Persuading older people to chat about, respond to, and think about their lives as older adults was easier than we had ever imagined it would be. We were at times stunned by the candor of the responses, by people's willingness to be vulnerable in noting their shortcomings as parents, spouses and partners, siblings, and friends, or to share how worried they were about their health, their sex lives, and, yes, the realization that they were in the fourth quarter of this journey of life. It became clear that, like us, most of our peers were unprepared for what they were encountering.

Every chapter of *Getting Real about Getting Older* contains poignant stories depicting the emotional and physical challenges of our respondents' lives. These are stories we are certain you will identify with while you think through your own painful and, yes, joyful issues. As you read through the Reality Check sections, consider the particular circumstances of your life and potential ways to cope better.

Our respondents were so eager to contribute to our project that many tracked us down after we spoke to them to tell us more. Others gave us their email addresses or phone numbers and asked to be kept informed about the progress of our book. They were eager to offer additional comments. They kept asking when our book would be completed so they could read it. They wanted advice *now*! Our respondents gave us insights into how to be older, *better*, and now we're sharing what we learned with you.

LINDA'S STORY

Like so many of our respondents, I never really imagined what I would look like as an old person or how I'd spend my time. Unlike other stages of my life, I had never really thought about getting old. I remember looking forward to meeting my spouse, to whom I've been married for more than fifty years. I especially looked forward to having children and grandchildren, getting my PhD, and landing that first awesome job. During those stages, I could articulate my goals, or at least know what to expect. But I was not prepared for being old. I knew I needed my doctorate to become a university professor, I knew I needed to write A-level journal articles to get tenure, and I knew I'd get kudos at work and maybe look cool in the eyes of my children when I appeared on the *NBC Nightly News*, was interviewed by Gayle King of *Oprah and Friends Radio*, and had my research highlighted in the *New York Times* and many other popular press news outlets. I planned for it all. I sought out the best universities to pursue my advanced degree and was accepted into Northwestern University, my first choice. I sought out information about every challenge that lay before me at every stage of my life. I read Dr. Spock and learned everything I could about being the best mom ever. But it *never, ever* dawned on me to learn about growing old. Then, suddenly, the years went by and I found myself undergoing not only physical changes evident of aging, but emotional changes as well.

I've traveled all over the world. Name a country, and I've probably been there, on my own, taking care of myself, and carrying my own bags. If a man offered to place my bag in the overhead bin, I felt a bit insulted. I was probably stronger than he, I reasoned. I went to the gym regularly, ran five miles most days, and could play tennis with the best of them. I didn't need someone helping me with my bags. However, it seemed that overnight, things changed. I was no longer as strong as the person asking to help me. I liked being offered a seat on the bus or subway. I appreciated having someone open the door for me.

I realize that I spend a lot of time thinking about growing old, that is, now that I finally get that I *am* old. I wonder why my relationships with my children seem to have changed. I wonder when I might have to give up my job and how that might play out. I even wonder who I really am now—now that a few of the many hats I've worn throughout my life have been removed. I don't think I ever really had time to *wonder* about much of anything before. I was too busy raising a family, being a mom, creating a career, and finding my place in the world. Now, I wonder a lot. Mostly…I wonder about getting older.

KAREN'S STORY

I was always the youngest in the group. With a January birthday and just making the cutoff date for kindergarten at four years and eight months, I was the youngest in my class, the youngest of my friends, the youngest wherever I went. It was something I came to expect and take for granted. My birthday was the last one to be celebrated in the class, and while there might have been some novelty to it at first, it became just part of who I was—Karen, the youngest. Even today, with my three closest friends, all of us over seventy, I am the youngest. But I'm not *young* anymore. I came to realize, sometime after I hit the half-century mark, that *young* is a relative term.

For a gymnast, twenty is old. For a football player, thirty-five is old and forty is ancient. For anything demanding physical stamina, youth has the honors, hands down. Nobody wants to look old, feel old, or *be* old. We all want to look young. It's a compliment when someone feigns surprise at hearing our age. "But you look so *young*," they say, lying through their teeth. "You sure don't *act* old," is another comment frequently heard. Actually, it's rather odd that we're so caught up in the youth culture when our youth makes up such a short period of our lives.

Adding to my ignorance of the relevance of age, I was an only child of older parents. My mother was in her early forties when I was born, and she was the youngest of seven. Everyone I knew in my family was old. I was surrounded by old people. It was my *normal*. With everyone else being old, and me being young, it was a complicated existence.

Then one day, somewhere around my sixty-fifth birthday,

there was no longer any reason to deny the cold, hard reality. All the old people in my life had passed on. I was alone, a female Davy Crockett holding down the Alamo of youth, doomed to defeat. I had to accept the fact that as I added candles to the cake each year, I was making slow but steady progress to the hall of fame of old people.

A glance in the mirror one day revealed someone who looked like my mother in her later years. It was a shock. When had I started resembling her? When did my laugh lines turn into creases that would rival glacial crevasses in the melting Arctic? When did the soft curve of my eyelids morph into crepe paper? And when did my neck become a network of folds that looked like a nesting place for wrens? It was a bit disconcerting, to say the least.

One day, I was old. And I found it fascinating. I was now one of the people I had grown up with. And, in an interesting way, life finally made sense. It was as if I had gained entrée into a world previously unknown to me. It promised to be a great adventure, and I was consumed with the desire to understand how others had come to this place. What were they thinking when they realized that, in the blink of an eye, they were old? What did it all mean? What *does* it all mean?

And so, with my friend, Linda, I set out on a quest to learn the answers to those questions. Age is a number, to be sure, but *aging*—ah, there's the real issue, isn't it? What does aging mean? This book was born from our desire to find the answers to the questions common to us all.

——— EVOLUTION OF THE BOOK ———

Our sons work together in San Mateo, California; that's how we met. We liked each other immediately, became friends, and worked together on a couple of projects. More and more often, our conversations turned to the fact that we were getting older, and how we might enjoy retirement yet stay relevant in our fields. How, we wondered, were other older people coping? How were they feeling about where they were in life? Were they better prepared than we were?

The stories we heard from our survey respondents and in our interviews and discussion groups were funny, poignant, and, above all, instructive. Some respondents feared they were becoming invisible. Fewer people seemed to listen to what they had to say. People weren't being intentionally rude, but our respondents realized they were often no longer part of the conversation. Their stories rang true to us. A slow and steady change was taking place. Were people no longer listening to us in the same ways they used to, or were we merely losing confidence in ourselves, as we could feel and see the physical and emotional changes occurring in our lives?

We became curious: What could we do to help others and ourselves grow older, *better*?

———— HISTORICAL UNDERCURRENTS ————

Some scientists define aging as a collection of changes that occur and render one more likely to die.[1] Geesh, really? What happened to that aging and fine wine concept?

There are multiple theories attempting to explain and develop a conceptual framework for the aging process. In the late 1800s, Darwinian theory—which gave us the idea of survival of the fittest—proposed that it was necessary for older people to remove themselves from the theater to make room for the next generation.[2] Turnover, it seemed, was an important part of a successful evolutionary process. Other theoretical explanations for the aging process support a *wear and tear* theory. According to this theory, just like our clothes, shoes, and furniture, people wear out and get replaced.[3]

Regardless of the aging theory in vogue today, of one thing we are certain. The major contrast between aging during the nineteenth century and today is a vast extension of the lifespan, thanks to medical advances, vaccines, nutrition, and healthier lifestyles. In the 1900s, a young boy could expect to live for 46.3 years and a young girl for 48.3 years. In contrast, today, a young boy can expect to live to be 76.3 and a young girl to be 81.2. On average, humans have gained an additional thirty-plus years of life since the beginning of the twentieth century. Deciding what to do with those thirty bonus years is the big question.[4] Indeed, today, many older people no longer are merely passive observers of their lives and have found ways to make good use of these added years. They're active participants in causes they believe in and in activities they enjoy. Many still are working well into their eighties.

Older people also represent a larger sector of society than they did in the past. The number of people of retirement age has grown from 7.5 million in the 1930s (when Social Security legislation came into effect and sixty-five was proclaimed the age of retirement) and will grow to nearly 55 million by 2020.[5]

We now know there is no need to remove the elderly from the theater. We can build a bigger theater and easily patch up those sitting in the seats. And we do. We patch up the elderly with heart transplants, knee and hip replacements, pacemakers, and even plastic surgery.

In short, older people are not letting their final years pass them by. Many continue to be active contributors to society and the economy well into their later years. Many are working to change the notion that aging is a frivolous time of life, when in fact it can be a time to give back through volunteer work and concerted, positive activities.

—— **WHY THIS BOOK IS IMPORTANT** ——

Getting older has a profound impact on every facet of our lives: our physical bodies, our sense of well-being, and our world view. It can even challenge our core beliefs about who we are and our value as human beings. Yet, most of us are woefully unprepared to effectively handle the transition to this stage of our lives. The need is greater than ever for a book from the perspective of the elderly, a book that helps readers under-stand the impact of these dramatic physical, emotional, and psychological changes. We hope the suggestions we offer in *Getting Real about Getting Older* will help older people—and younger people preparing for older age—walk a more positive path through the final years of their lives.

GETTING *Real* ABOUT GETTING OLDER

Chapter 1

IF I COULD TURN BACK TIME...

"If you think you can do at sixty-seven what you did at twenty-five, chances are you were not doing much at twenty-five."

—ANONYMOUS

One of the questions we asked the participants in our survey was: "What surprised you most about growing older?" The most frequent response hands down was that they had aged so fast. They simply couldn't believe they were *old*. They felt much, much younger than they were. An overriding concern was that time was going too fast—now that they were old, they feared they couldn't get everything done (even in a day) that they had hoped they would. They feared that time was running out.

— IT'S AS IF ONE DAY, YOU'RE JUST OLD —

Many respondents told us that they had felt pretty much the same age for most of their adult lives. Their faces and bodies might have changed slightly, but the mental image they had of themselves had changed very little.

At some point, however, they realized they were *elderly*. They felt and looked different for sure, and they thought differently about many things. Some said it seemed as if they had just awakened one day in a different body.

It strikes us as curious that becoming older takes so many of us by surprise. We all know older people, and we see older people on TV (but, come to think of it, not too many), yet we tend to think that *we* will never be old. It seems that many of us think we will stay young forever. Then, one day, we realize that we aren't moving as quickly as we used to. Minor injuries take longer to heal. We're not as strong or as mobile as we used to be. While most of us experience these changes gradually, the overall impression is that *time went so fast*!

It seems like I just woke up one day and I was seventy-two. I guess I should have known it was going to happen, but most times, I just can't believe it. I feel much younger. I wish I had known this was going to happen to me. I might have made better use of my younger years. It's not even that I might have done anything differently or made different choices, I would have just more fully enjoyed being young. As I look at the current crinkles and wrinkles in my body, I would have more fully realized my body wasn't so bad after all.

—Seventy-two-year-old crinkled woman

It happened so quickly. For me, aging seemed to happen overnight. One day I could keep up with my son as we rode bikes through the hills and valleys of San Francisco. The next day, I was having a hip replacement. How did I not see that coming?

—Sixty-eight-year-old caught-off-guard professor

I know it must seem hard to believe, but I don't think I ever really thought I would be an older person. I didn't think I would die young or anything like that. I have just never imagined myself as an older person. I could imagine myself as a parent, as a manager, or as a spouse, but I have never imagined myself as an older person.

—Seventy-year-old number cruncher

When we finally acknowledge that we're old—whether at sixty-five, seventy, or older—time continues to move rapidly. In fact, as we get older, time seems to go by faster than ever before.

Of course, although we may feel that time is flying by, it isn't moving any faster than it did at any other point in our lives. One hypothesis for this change in perception is that our biological clock slows as we age.[6] While we are slowing down physically, we perceive that the rest of our world is speeding up. This sensation can partially be explained by the fact that it takes older people longer to do things than it used to, and as a result, they feel time is passing quickly.

It's not just our older respondents who observe this. Changes in the perception of time as we age is a topic of interest to writers and researchers as well. Experiments have shown that older people really do perceive time as going faster, as compared to younger people. In her book *Time Warped*, Claudia Hammond recounts an experiment in which twenty-year-olds and seventy-year-olds were asked to indicate when a minute had passed, without counting the seconds. The seventy-year-olds were less accurate than the twenty-year-olds. A *minute* seemed to go by a lot more quickly for the seventy-year-olds.

When we look back at our lives, certain events stand out. As we grow up, there are many things for us to accomplish. There are skills to learn, people to meet, milestones to reach (first crush, first job, first everything). So many memorable moments are crammed into the early part of our lives.

I can clearly remember the big events of life: getting married, starting/buying businesses, births, deaths. But the everyday of life passes in a blur. Those events in my life were memorable. It seems as though I have fewer big memorable events now that I am older, fewer "markers" in my life.

—Seventy-three-year-old used-to-be entrepreneur

As our respondent noted, as we age, the number of new and memorable events decreases. We can only do something for the first time once, and as the gaps between these big events increase, we fill in these gaps with less memorable events and activities. As a result, time seems to be going faster.

I guess the best analogy I can think of is the toilet paper roll. You know how when it gets down near the end, it seems to go so much faster. Well, I feel just like that toilet paper roll, now that I'm getting near the end, my life seems to be going so much faster.

—Sixty-nine-year-old mountain man

Of course, the toilet paper roll really does go faster as the circumference of the roll decreases, but for our sixty-nine-year-old mountain man, it was an important analogy.

Psychologist Jean Piaget coined the term *schema* to

describe how our brains categorize events in order to store and retrieve information more easily.[7] The first time we have an experience, he wrote, we remember it with greater detail because of its novelty. We're less likely to remember subsequent similar events with such detail, and we assign fewer memorable markers between each experience. Fewer life-changing events tend to occur as we get older, which gives the illusion that time has passed more quickly, given we have so little to show for the time that has passed.

☞ REALITY CHECK

Anticipating an upcoming event gives us the perception that time is moving more slowly; similarly, events that we dread seem to last a long time, while we perceive fun or exciting things to go by quickly. If you want to increase your perception that time is moving less quickly, do more and stay more active.

1. What events have you experienced that you can picture vividly? When did they occur? Should you plan more "firsts?"

2. What events have you experienced recently that were life-changing? Can you describe them in great detail?

3. What activities or events would you consider planning that could be life-changing, or at least something you could anticipate and look forward to?

—— IT'S ALL IN HOW YOU PERCEIVE IT ——

The degree of importance we place on any specific year in our lives, and on time itself, is based on the total amount of time we have lived. For example, one year in a five-year-old's life is 20 percent of her lifetime (a relatively long time) while one year is less than 2 percent (a relatively short time) in the life of a seventy-year-old. Researchers have determined that the relative importance of that one year, therefore, differs greatly depending on how old a person is.[8]

Our respondents told us that they feel time has become less important as they've grown older—less important in the sense that they can get up when they want, go to bed when they want, eat when they want. They're not controlled by the clock in any way, aside from the occasional dentist appointment. For the most part, they set their own schedules. And sometimes they aren't even sure what day it is.

Many of our respondents felt stressed because to them, time seems to be going by so quickly. Yet, there is no need to feel anxious. It's simply the perception of reality, not reality itself. To ensure fewer instances when it seems as if time is flying by, take a deep breath and try to live in the moment. Then consider the wise advice of this respondent:

"Seize the Carp!" I saw this on a car bumper sticker and thought it was perfect. Kind of an inside joke. Yes, I know the right words (carpe diem), but "seizing the carp" seems like a lot more fun and a lot more doable than trying to lasso twenty-four hours.

It's all about living in the present. The now. That's all we have, if you think about it. Today. And an entire day is quite a bit of time if you live it the best you can. Nobody's guaranteed tomorrow, and whatever you did yesterday is in the past. Living there doesn't make much sense. It's nice to visit the past and recall pleasant times, and it's also nice to think about the future. Making plans is a great way to pass some time. But when all is said and done, this moment, this second, will never come again, and it's just as precious when you're seventy as when you're seven.

—Seventy-year-old word processor

☞ REALITY CHECK

Research tells us that time is measured by the number of memorable events in your life, so becoming more active should slow down your perception of time. If you do more, see more, and have more experiences, your days, months, and years will seem longer. They will certainly be richer.

You're at the time in your life, or soon will be, when you can try something challenging and do what you've always wanted to do but never had the time for. This doesn't mean you have to take an exotic trip to Africa or a boat ride to China, although if you have the means and the stamina, these may be attractive options. As a start, consider these possibilities:

1. Try a new hobby. If you've golfed all your life, try fly fishing; if you play tennis, try sailing; if you've always read novels, try reading a biography of someone you admire, or better yet, of someone you've never heard of.

2. Do something that requires effort.

3. Get out of your routine.

4. Make new friends.

5. Discover the rewards of volunteering.

6. Keep learning.

7. Expand your horizons, and time will expand to meet you as well.

BETTER LATE THAN NEVER

"I am old, and the old are not wanted, and what they say has no weight."

—THE GRANDFATHER IN *MOONSTRUCK*

In the movie *Moonstruck* (1987), Loretta (played by Cher) is widowed and about to remarry when she falls in love with her fiancé's younger brother, Ronny (Nicholas Cage). Her father (Vincent Gardenia) doesn't want to pay for a second wedding, but her grandfather (Feodor Chaliapin Jr.) disagrees, prefacing his case with the line quoted above.

Loretta's grandfather knows his situation is not a good one. He's living in his son's house. He has nothing except his dogs and a family that tolerates him out of a sense of responsibility. He hangs out at the cemetery, and that is his life, visiting the graves of friends and relatives. He has little to no independence. It's not that his family doesn't love him; they just don't seem to respect him anymore.

Our respondents expressed similar feelings about the perception of the elderly. They felt they often are not honored, respected, or valued, and are considered a burden.

So, back to the old man in *Moonstruck*. He obviously is a victim of his old age. He clings to the idea that he's still the head of his family. He hasn't accepted the present reality, nor has he made choices that would give him a better life. His life and his world have gotten smaller and smaller. His life is stereo-typically that of an old person. Although it may not seem so, he has choices; he's just not considering them.

Now imagine for a moment how this character's life would be different if he accepted his circumstances and took charge of his life. He eventually does this. In somewhat of an epiphany, he comes to understand that if he wants to be heard, he must have something of value to say. He examines his conscience and realizes that he has let his family down. He asks himself where he went wrong with his family, with his son, and he is forced to accept the fact that the blame is his. He begins to *man up*. He realizes he has refused to exact respect from his family, and, as he once again begins to reassert himself, refusing to be silenced, the respect returns and order is restored to the family.

Live in the present. It's good advice. Seek out opportu-nities to live life and make better use of the precious time you have left. Instead of just existing or daydreaming of years past, make the conscious decision to get back in the game of life.

☞ REALITY CHECK

There is no time like the present to choose a better life for yourself. If you're waiting for someone else to do it for you, it's not going to happen. You might ask yourself these questions:

1. What are your barriers to creating a new life? Are they real or perceived? Are you tied to your community? Could you make a move, even if temporarily? Could you do a house swap with someone from a different country for a summer?

2. Do you need to redefine yourself? In the next chapter, we discuss the need to redefine your identity as you get older. For now, ask yourself: Have you moved on from the person you were when you were younger? How do you imagine yourself in the future? Do you even recognize that you still have a future, not just a past?

3. When you've decided to take on something new, don't give up until you've succeeded! What can you do to make this a reality?

We often make valiant attempts to change our lives. We strive to be more health-conscious, to learn a new language, to have new experiences. The important reality check here is not to be afraid to tackle the unknown. Don't overthink your challenges. Don't get bogged down in fearing that you won't succeed. Just make up your mind to *do it*! Again, our respondents offered sage advice.

"Just passing through"—this is my mantra. It keeps me from getting too caught up in the minutiae of life. I'm trying to focus on the bigger picture. There's so much to see and do in this life, and if I only have one shot at it, I want to keep my eyes open so I don't miss a thing.

—Seventy-year-old golfer

I have the sense of movement, even when I'm at rest. You know, that "time is a river" thing? That's what I'm talking about. We're all on a journey. It begins the day we're born and never stops until we draw our final breath. It's all about motion. Going forward toward some goal still to be determined.

—Seventy-three-year-old with a new voice

I don't ever remember being this "aware" of my life—that the years are flying by, that my days are truly numbered, that my kids will one day go on without me. I even try to think what life will be like without me on this earth, when I realize...it will just go on.

—Eighty-three-year-old beauty

A pebble tossed in a pond creates ripples, but those ripples quickly fade away and the surface of the pond becomes smooth again. We are the pebbles in the pond of life, and everything we do creates ripples. Just as with the pond, however, time will continue, and life will go on after we're gone. While we're here, though, we need to make the most of it.

By now, you can see that you're not alone in feeling that the years are slipping by faster than ever; all older folks have a real sense of the shortening of time. We all are immensely, even painfully, aware that we have less time left to live than we have already lived. If we're living a life we're happy with, that's fine; if not, there are options. The choices are ours to make. As the old man in *Moonstruck* realized, it's better late than never.

In the meantime:

- Recognize that enjoying your later years is an active process, not a passive one.

- Understand that you can still make choices to make your life better.
- Begin living. You can't turn back time, but you can wind up the clock and get ready for tomorrow.

Chapter 2

NOW YOU SEE ME, NOW YOU DON'T

"I am invisible, understand, simply because people refuse to see me."

—RALPH ELLISON

W e may not remember the first time we experienced invisibility, and we're not sure how to label it. It's something akin to loneliness. It's that moment when we first realize people aren't really listening to us anymore. It doesn't happen to everyone, of course, and not in every situation, but it happens from time to time and it's troubling. So, what's the deal with invisibility? It shows itself in a variety of subtle and not-so-subtle slights, from being ignored in conversations to finding ourselves referred to in the third person while we're standing right there, big as life. As we age, we seem to have a more difficult time getting people to pay attention to what we have to say. When we speak, our words may not be acknowledged. It's as if nobody hears us. We're overlooked in a meeting or group or family setting. It isn't that others are being rude or purposely ignoring us. They simply do not recognize that we are part of the ongoing discussion or, for that matter, that we are even there.[9] And so, we may find ourselves retreating, our voices silenced.

There is no simple explanation for why this happens, although much of the blame can be placed on our youth-oriented (some might say youth-obsessed) culture. Also, we have become an impatient society. Everything moves fast. There is no time for reflection to process all the sensory inputs we're bombarded with. Older people may move more slowly than the young, and given the fast pace of life today, there just isn't the patience for the older members of society to catch up. Fashion, entertainment, even the latest handheld tech devices with their small keyboards that are difficult for arthritic hands to use—everything is geared toward the young. Also, it's possible that older people may make some younger adults uncomfortable. The elderly are reminders of how fleeting life is, evoking fear in younger people who don't want to be reminded of their own mortality.

Nearly all of our respondents indicated that they've experienced the awkwardness of feeling invisible. Making ourselves visible can be a big challenge, but there are ways to do it. It takes a little finesse, a little effort, and an awareness that we have control over the situation. The difference between being visible and invisible comes down to two letters—*in*. We've got to actively decide to put ourselves back *in* the picture.

What I've noticed as I've gotten older is the difference in the way various individuals treat you. The treatment can range from deference to disregard. Many clerks, some medical personnel, and others see gray hair, some wrinkles, and immediately assume that you don't know what you are talking about. It requires extra effort to convince these people that you indeed know what you are talking about, and they need to listen to what you are saying. The good news is grandchildren, on the other hand, are more apt to regard you as a fountain of wisdom.

—Sixty-five-year-old disregarded grandma

For the first time in my life, I understand what it must be like for some women and minorities. I'm ignored, my opinion really doesn't matter to most, and I often feel invisible unless I'm with people of my own age.

—Seventy-one-year-old invisible guy

From deference to disregard—that's a wide range of ways you might find yourself being ignored, and it highlights the complexity of this conundrum. In times past, gray hair and wrinkles indicated experience and some hard-won wisdom from which younger people could benefit. Society has changed a lot since those days, and, more and more, we worship at the altar of the fountain of youth. As those of us with the gray hair and wrinkles can attest, however, the fountain of youth is an illusion, and the worship is misplaced.

EXPECT THE UNEXPECTED, AND EMBRACE IT

I got one of those survey phone calls last night. The young woman asked to speak to the head of the house. I told her she was. Then she asked me if I were over sixty. I said I was. She thanked me and told me they were looking for younger people. I'd just been snubbed by a telephone survey taker. How desperate does that make me sound?

—Sixty-eight-year-old not-so-young man

Honestly, who could have seen that one coming? We do our best to get out of conversations with telemarketers, but we're not used to doing it on their terms. It's the ultimate rebuff. When they hang up simply because we're *too old*—it surprises us. As does our shock when we are filling out any array of forms and we find that seventy, eighty, or older isn't even a category on a form—we're all lumped into sixty-five and older!

Forewarned is forearmed, however. It's important to realize that what you perceive as an insult may not have been meant to be one. Suppose the survey-taker had been looking for owners of basset hounds or people with type A negative blood? Would you have been offended if you didn't fit that profile? Probably not. At least, the caller thanked our respondent. The takeaway? *Don't take offense where none is intended.* Once we have developed the perception that we are invisible, we must guard against feeling invisible in every discussion, situation, or personal interaction where it may not exist. We must ask ourselves if we're really being ignored, or if it's our own insecurities and self-doubt coming into play to make the interaction seem more offensive than it should be.

Sometimes our overreactions are rooted in a perceived loss of power or in not feeling needed or in the recognition that we can no longer do some things. Everyone wants to feel needed, but as we get older there may be an increasing number of occasions when our roles are no longer necessary. In some ways this can be liberating. To not constantly be needed or be on somebody's *go-to* list means there's more time to do what we want. As with most things in life, though, striking a balance is important. To not be needed by anyone, ever, can be a recipe for a very lonely existence, but that doesn't have to happen. *Find a need and fill it* is good advice, regardless of our age. To do this right, we've got to stop thinking about ourselves first and think of others instead. Those who do are always needed. It might be easy for a cynic to say, "Sure, there's always somebody worse off than I am. I could be dead." That's true. But we're not dead, and we have talents and gifts to share with others.

Last night we went to our community's annual "Mystery Theatre" event. It was the first time I bought a ticket instead of manning the ticket booth. It was the first time I enjoyed a glass of punch and a cookie without worrying about keeping the tables filled. And it was the first time I actually got to enjoy the entire presentation without wondering if I'd ordered enough trash containers for the cleanup afterward. I'd either chaired or served on all of these committees over the years. Truly, a burden lifted. Others had taken over these tasks. I was free to totally enjoy myself.

—Sixty-seven-year-old liberated committee person

☞ REALITY CHECK

Think back to a time when your talents, wisdom, and help were appreciated. What were the circumstances? How can you reconnect to that sense of feeling valued?

Need some examples to help you break out of the invisibility mode? They abound.

1. Love animals? Contact your local animal shelter. Shelters cannot operate without volunteers, from people who answer the phone to those who collect donations and socialize animals in need.

2. Skilled at carpentry or home repair? How about helping less-mobile seniors by installing grab rails and other assistive devices around the home? Contact your local senior center for further information or for ideas of other worthwhile opportunities. We promise they won't hang up on you.

3. Enjoy sewing or quilting or knitting? Hospitals welcome donations of caps and layettes for preemies. And there's the 1 Million Pillowcase Challenge, which provides colorful and comforting pillowcases for needy children.[10]

4. If that feeling of being invisible surfaces, ask yourself, are you really being ignored, or are your own insecurities and self-doubt just coming into play? Regardless of what exactly they are, begin to busy yourself with fulfilling activities that increase your self-confidence.

If you're feeling superfluous, unnecessary, and unappreciated, you can change that scenario beginning with an attitude adjustment. Don't let your horizons shrink just because you're adding years to your life. Focus on adding some life to your years.

UNDERSTAND THE SITUATION

I was on a road trip with some buddies and we pulled up to this rest area. There was a bunch of people gathered around, watching a guy taking his bike apart. He had tools and parts all around him, and it seemed to be pretty clear he didn't have a clue what to do with them. My buddy's a mechanic, so he goes over to the guy and asks him if he needs some help. The guy looks up—right past my buddy—and asks this young guy next to me if he's got a metric tool kit. He's got some weird fitting and he's missing what he needs.

My buddy shrugs and we leave. I made some comment, but
my buddy just said, "It happens."

—Sixty-eight-year-old dissed mechanic's friend

What's going on here? At first glance, the young man with
the bike problem seems to ignore the older man in the group
when he offers to help. To the older guys, the biker just seems
rude as he appears to look for someone his own age to help him
and ignores the older man's offer. Why is this happening?

There's a lot going on here, and there are a lot of assump-
tions. The older man assumes that the younger man doesn't
know what he is doing, and maybe that comes through in his
tone of voice when he offers to help. The young man is preoccu-
pied with his repairs. He knows what he needs, but it is missing.
He looks up and connects with someone he thinks will be able
to give him what he needs. He doesn't want help; he wants a
tool. So why does he ignore the offer of help? Maybe he didn't
even hear it. Maybe he hears the offer, but he is afraid the
older man will take over. Subconsciously, maybe he is assert-
ing his independence from his father! Then again, maybe he
is just plain rude and doesn't believe that an older man would
be able to help him. Our respondent's friend shrugs off the
slight, but it's apparent from his comment, "It happens," that
he feels invisible, even if just a little. Should he? Perhaps he

misperceived the whole situation and let his own growing lack of self-confidence force him to be less objective than he could have been.

Realistically, ignoring the offer to help may have been deliberate. Age discrimination does exist. So, what is the snubbed mechanic to do? If he and his buddy weren't in a hurry, perhaps just hanging around a bit longer would have taken the edge off. Taking time to assess the situation before jumping in with a solution might have allowed the older man to come across as interested without looking as if he wanted to take charge. Regardless of your age, nobody appreciates a latecomer barging in with a solution to a problem. Go slow. The first comment shouldn't be a solution. It should be a compliment: "I had a bike just like yours. I learned a lot on it. Had some great rides."

In this case, though, the mechanic replied, "It happens." If he's experiencing this kind of snubbing frequently, maybe it's time to take a serious look at how he comes across. A softer approach in many situations might pay off.

Not everyone is going to want what you have to offer. This is always true, regardless of your age. So how can you best help others without getting hurt in the process? One way is to go online to connect with others. There are email Listservs and websites for people with every hobby imaginable, from boating to woodworking, to antique cars, to hunting and fishing, to firearms, to quilting, to knitting, to dryer lint collecting. The list goes on and on, and if you have limited mobility or live in an area where you don't have the opportunity to share your skills, you will open a door to the world. You'll meet people from all walks of life and all age groups. There are no borders and no limitations. Find a group (or groups) that interest you and join them. Every day, people post questions, ask for help with problems, look for sources for materials, and share what they've learned. They're actively seeking out people with knowledge. The key here is that when you're online, age is irrelevant. Nobody asks or cares how old you are. The only thing that matters is your expertise. You've amassed a lifetime of experiences and learned from them. This is your chance to share what you know to an appreciative audience. In essence, it's the master-apprentice relationship updated for the twenty-first century. You'll be helping others and you'll be *visible*.

I've been a boater most of my life, and I belong to a trawler Listserv that's a great forum for sharing information and solutions to problems with other boaters. One guy was having issues with installation of a new toilet in the head. The thread went on for days. Everybody was sharing their experiences with similar problems. Some of them were funny, and some of them were technical. I look forward to reading this feed every day with my morning coffee. Sometimes, I offer my own advice. It's a great group.

—Seventy-year-old advice-giver

Another way to share your knowledge and skills is to contact your local parks and recreation department. Every summer they have programs to teach young people various skills—everything from making birdhouses to flying kites to photography, and often they're looking for experienced adults to lead those kinds of classes.

For year-round opportunities, check out 4-H programs through your local county extension service, Boy Scouts, or Girl Scouts. Your skills are needed, and you don't have to limit your social interactions to people your own age. Living is about growing. You either grow bigger or you grow smaller. If you want to break out of the invisibility trap, take charge and make the decision to grow bigger.

— DON'T APOLOGIZE FOR BEING OLDER —

The saleswoman at the dress shop actually told me I was too old to wear a dress that had caught my eye. She said the color was much too bright for me and she wanted to show me something in a darker gray or brown. The dress was a lovely shade of royal blue. It had a silver thread running through it, and it was just what I had been looking for. I told her I was definitely not too old for it, and in fact, I was going to also get it in red. And for the record, I'm eighty-two.

—Eighty-two-year-old colorful gal

In this situation, the only reason our respondent was being told she was too old to wear the dress she wanted was simply because the sales clerk had firm ideas about what was an appropriate color for an older woman to wear, and her belief that older women should blend in and be *invisible*. By standing up for herself, the woman asserted her independence, became visible, and we hope taught the clerk a valuable lesson. This visibility problem was about *color*. In case you were absent the day they covered proper color choices for older women, it apparently went like this:

Good: Darker colors.

Bad: Brighter colors.

Pretty simple. Pretty stupid. The truth: Wear whatever color you like. If it looks good on you, you score bonus points.

Act your age is probably an expression you've heard

countless times as you've been negotiating this journey through life. It makes sense to a large degree, which is undoubtedly why the expression has been around so long. *Act your age* is usually an admonishment. It's a way of correcting people's behavior by reminding them that there are certain behaviors expected at specific life markers and they're not living up to society's expectations. If there were no societal norms for behaviors, there would be chaos. That is why teens who throw temper tantrums are told to act their age and not behave like two-year-olds. In the same vein, older adults who try to fit in with a younger crowd by adopting the current youth slang don't cut it. They're abandoning their peer group and trying to join a younger one. They're not acting their age; they're acting desperate.

Generally, *act your age* refers to behaviors. It's easy to carry this one step further, however, and translate that to how to dress. Should there be a uniform for older folks? Colorful Gal says definitely not. She knows what she likes, she looks good in it, and she asserts her right to dress as she pleases.[11]

Continuing the theme of fashion choices, our next respondent wasn't comfortable wearing sleeveless outfits any longer. It was her decision, based on what she thought looked best on her. Nobody was telling her what she should or shouldn't be wearing.

I gave up on sleeveless dresses the day I nearly gave myself a black eye with my underarm. I'd reached up to grab something off the top shelf and that part of my arm got to swinging so hard I thought it would get airborne. After that I stuck to cap sleeves and longer. My swinging wings are now my own little secret.

—Seventy-eight-year-old swinging-wings gal

Adapting to reality isn't giving in to aging. It's using common sense. On the one hand, our eighty-two-year-old respondent's choice of red and blue dresses reflects her self-confidence. She has no plans to be invisible. On the other hand, our seventy-eight-year-old who chooses to dress to disguise what she *perceives* to be a less-than-attractive feature of her body reflects self-confidence as well. She knows what type of clothing makes her comfortable. She's in charge of what she wears.

Men have it a bit easier than women in the fashion department. Once men retire, they leave the uniforms of their former occupations behind, usually with satisfaction, and wear whatever they feel like, as long as it's comfortable. If they are criticized for their choices, it's often because they haven't bought new clothes since leisure suits were in style.

Men aren't traditionally labeled by what they wear, but

rather by what they do, or as they get older and retire, what they *did*. That's a topic we'll cover more fully in a later chapter.

Sometimes it takes all my energy to make the effort to get dressed up and go out. Nobody really looks at me anymore. I could be wearing a polka dot clown suit and it wouldn't make any difference. Inside I'm still me, but I'm old and nobody really sees me.

—Sixty-five-year-old could-be-a-polka-dotted clown

Remember those days of your youth when you agonized over every facial blemish, positive that the whole world was staring at you and your imperfection? It hurt. A lot. Happily, there is a freedom that comes with getting older, and you may find that your physical appearance is less of a source of angst as you age. Regardless, you may feel self-conscious about your wrinkles and other signs of aging and wish to have your younger body back. We sometimes want it both ways, but life doesn't work like that. Yes, you were young once. Now you're old. The whole world wasn't staring at your zit when you were fourteen, and they're not staring at you now—that is, unless you *do* decide to wear a polka dot clown suit. The real issue here is self-worth. What you wear is a reflection of how you feel about yourself. If you are comfortable in your own skin, nobody is going to convince you to wear shapeless, colorless clothing. If you aren't comfortable with yourself, then nothing you wear will make you feel good.

Self-worth is one of the most precious possessions we have. As we get older and less is needed from us or our help or ideas are no longer appreciated, it can be difficult to maintain a healthy self-esteem. That is why the suggestions we mentioned earlier of how to connect with people who share your interests and need your wisdom are vitally important to keeping your self-esteem high and your sense of self-worth supported.

My mother had two rules she hammered into our heads: Dress Up and Show Up. She believed that if you took the time to make yourself look your best, you'd do better at everything all day long. I forgot a lot of what other people have told me throughout my life, but her words got me through Pee Wee football, basic training, and my MBA program. She was the reason I outperformed others' expectations of me. I didn't hold back. I made others see me. Even now, I'm retired but I still consult. And I still dress up every day. Even when I don't feel like it. It's a habit and I couldn't break it if I tried.

—Sixty-eight-year-old dresses-up-and-shows-up guy

The takeaway here is that getting older doesn't require you to stop shaving, brushing your teeth, putting on clean underwear, and shining your shoes. Granted, it may take you a little longer to get it all done, but the end result is worth it. You'll like yourself more, and you'll remind yourself to be *visible*. Do the prep work. Too often we get lazy when we no longer have to punch the time clock. We cut corners and get a bit sloppy or careless. The problem with that is that once we start down this slippery slope, being sloppy and careless gets easier and easier. There is a price to pay for this change in our appearance, and it's a decreased sense of self-worth. The bottom line is that if we don't care enough about ourselves to attend to grooming and cleanliness, we won't command respect from others. Pity, perhaps. Compassion, possibly. Respect, no. We have to respect ourselves first before we can expect others to take notice of us. There are days when it can take an effort to put on our best face and clean clothes, but the end result will do wonders for our self-confidence, and self-confident people are *visible*.

☞ REALITY CHECK

Consider these questions as you assess your own invisibility issues.

1. Have you experienced times when you felt you were being ignored or as if someone were talking past you to other people, as if you weren't there?

2. How could you have asserted yourself so that you weren't being overlooked?

3. Have you been with someone who was experiencing these same slights? What did you do?

4. What can you do the next time this happens? What will you say?

IF YOU DON'T GET RESPECT, FIGHT FOR IT

I was at the doctor's office. My daughter had driven me and had come into the waiting room with me. I have macular degeneration and had to give up my license. That was hard for me. It took a big chunk of my independence, but June is great about driving me where I need to go. I try to lump my appointments into the same day so we can go out to lunch together. I'm also mindful of the time it takes, and I don't want to impose on her. She's got a busy life. Anyhow, the medical assistant came over with a clipboard

that had some forms on it. She handed it to my daugh-
ter! I took the clipboard and told her I was the patient,
not my daughter. The woman just smiled and winked at
my daughter. I was so mad. I wish I'd had some smart
comeback, but you never think of one until you're back
home again. I mean, really. Am I invisible or something?
Do I look that incompetent?

—Seventy-five-year-old not-so-patient patient

This is a case of justifiable anger. Unfortunately, this type of treatment is extremely common, and people who are assisted by power chairs or wheelchairs experience such lack of respect on a regular basis, no matter their age. Often, the behavior is a subconscious reaction that's a result of the person in the chair appearing shorter, and hence, smaller than an erect adult. Adults who appear smaller may be perceived as childlike and not competent or able to speak for themselves. Perhaps the perception also exists that the appearance of being smaller means your mental abilities are limited. The assumption is that if the body isn't functioning all that well, the mind must not be either. That doesn't justify the behavior, however. Medical staff need to be trained to communicate directly with the patient unless they are given other instructions.

Analyzing our respondent's comments on this topic gives us some good points to consider. Nothing ever happens in a vacuum. There are many factors in play in any given situation, and no situation is ever as easy as it appears at first glance. So, in the situation above, what's actually going on?

Our respondent had to give up her driver's license. She had been driving since she was sixteen—that's over half a century of independence behind the wheel, and she's never going to get that level of independence back. Her vision is deteriorating and will continue to worsen. She's frightened about losing more than the ability to drive to the grocery store—she's afraid that someday she won't even be able to see what she has bought at the grocery store. There's also a role reversal in progress. Her daughter is becoming the caregiver. This isn't an easy change in circumstances for the older woman to accept or maybe even acknowledge. Still, she's perfectly able to speak for herself and give directions to people who are assisting her. It's important for her self-concept and self-worth to remain as independent as possible.

The medical assistant erred on two counts. This happened at the ophthalmologist's office. Even if the assistant knew the respondent's vision was compromised, she should have greeted the patient first and offered her the clipboard. This would have given the respondent the option to either fill out the forms herself or to ask her daughter to help with the task.

By bypassing the patient, the medical assistant made our respondent feel invisible and assumed that the daughter was the responsible party. The second error was one of simple rudeness. Winking at the daughter as if the respondent were a small child trying to act like a grownup is unforgivable.

The daughter also could have behaved more respectfully toward her mother. Instead of accepting the clipboard when the assistant handed it to her, she should have kept her hands to her sides and simply stated, "My mother is here to see the doctor. I'm her daughter." Instead of passively accepting the conspiratorial wink, she should have called the assistant on it on the spot. "Excuse me, do you have something in your eye?" would have gotten the message across plainly and simply.

Finally, our respondent did not respond as assertively as she could have. After taking a deep breath, she should have informed the doctor of the way she had been treated. Good doctors want to know what is going on in their practices. If nobody tells them when something is egregiously wrong, they can't fix it. And the next time she goes to the doctor's office, she should be prepared to be an advocate for herself. This can be difficult when you're not feeling well, but you'll feel a whole lot better when you're treated with the respect you deserve.

———— **CALL YOUR OWN SHOTS** ————

We used to go to the movies every Saturday, my husband and I. We really looked forward to it. We'd go out to dinner and a movie and then take a walk along the seashore before going home. It was one of those happy traditions. But they just don't seem to make films for older folks any more. They're short on plot, loud, and vulgar. And except for the "geezer" films where they do some sort of reunion of every actor over the age of sixty doing some impossible action roles—you know, the ones where they save the planet or something and rescue a young woman with big breasts and martial arts skills—it's almost impossible to find an older cast. Some of the British films are good, but there's not much made for our age group any more. It's as if we don't even exist.

—Sixty-five-year-old lookin'-for-a-movie gal

I stopped looking at the tabloids after Elizabeth Taylor died. I don't know anybody on the covers anymore. I don't care about the people they write about, and they don't care about me as a reader.

—Seventy-five-year-old Elizabeth Taylor lover

Both of our respondents are spot on about the limited representation of older people in popular culture. And nothing is going to change. Making movies is all about making money. Older people don't go to the movies because there are so few movies being made for them. Since they don't go to the movies much anymore, fewer and fewer movies are made for them. It's a vicious cycle. So, does this mean that the entire older demographic is invisible to Hollywood? Essentially, yes.[12]

According to the Motion Picture Association of America's 2016 Theatrical Market Statistics report, twenty-five- to thirty-nine-year-olds constituted the largest share of movie-goers in 2016, at 23 percent. Adults sixty and older comprised less than 15 percent. Those statistics are not surprising, considering the way seniors are represented in both film and television. Doris Roberts, best known for her role as Marie Barone on the TV show *Everybody Loves Raymond*, summed up the situation in a 2003 interview with the Parents Television Council: "[Seniors] do not see themselves portrayed and when they do, it's in a demeaning manner. They're referred to as 'over the hill,' 'old goats,' and 'old farts'—oh please, ugly ways of talking about us."

As an older person, you may be invisible to Hollywood, but that's the industry's problem. They're invisible to you as well. Call it a standoff, while recognizing that you have other options when it comes to entertainment.

Just because our movie gal and her husband have been going out to the movies every Saturday doesn't mean they can't adopt a new Saturday routine. Traditions can be broken and new ones embraced.

Every year for Christmas, we give each other a boxed set of an old television series. We watch one episode a night at cocktail hour. It's great fun looking at them, and since it's been years and years since we've seen them, it's like watching a new show every night with familiar characters. We've watched Mannix; Cannon; The Streets of San Francisco; The Rockford Files; Magnum, P.I.; Rawhide—*so many good shows. We'll have another couple over and make a movie night of it.*

—Eighty-year-old *Rockford Files* lover

There's an added benefit to adopting a fun, new movie routine like this one. By watching the movie in the quiet of your own home, you avoid sticky theater floors and gummy seats, overpriced popcorn, and people talking on their phones, and you can adjust the sound level to suit your hearing—or lack of it. And many older films (and newer ones increasingly) are available for free online.

☞ REALITY CHECK

Accepting changes in your circumstances can be difficult. Many times, these changes are permanent. You
can't regain your youth, but you can choose to live
your later years the best way you possibly can.

1. What are some of the changes you've noticed
    in yourself as you've aged?

2. Are you comfortable with these changes? If you
    are, how did you reach that comfort level?

3. If you're not comfortable with the changes
    that older life has brought, what can you do to
    make your situation better?

4. Denial and resistance aren't effective coping
    tools; rather, adaptation is the key to success-
    ful aging.

— WHAT HAPPENED TO MY SEX APPEAL? —

*I never gave a thought to the day when I'd no longer be
sexually attractive. I mean, everything seems to revolve
around sex. Everything a woman wears, puts on her face or*

her hair, or the jewelry she wears is meant to enhance her sex appeal. Finding out I no longer had any was a bit unsettling. Back when I was a girl, I'd walk past construction sites and the wolf whistles were something I came to expect. I enjoyed that. Feeling sexy is nice. But now, nothing. When it's over, it's over.

—Sixty-five-year-old wanting-a-wolf-whistle gal

We're sexual beings. Nature has designed humans to be mutually attracted, with one goal and one goal only in mind: reproduction of the species. It's in the best interest of the species for men and women to crave the other. Life revolves around sexual desire, and without it, we wouldn't exist. How we feel and act on our sexual feelings as we get older depends, as it does at other times in our lives, on the circumstances.

Many women begin to feel their sex appeal waning and that they're becoming invisible sexually when they begin menopause. This change of life is a wake-up call that their bodies are changing dramatically. Indeed, once upon a time, menopause marked more than the end of the monthly menstrual cycle, it marked the end of life itself. The two essentially coincided. Once a woman's capability for reproduction ended, nature had no further need of her and she would likely

Anythink Bennett

495 7th Street
Bennett, CO 80102
303-405-3231
Tues and Thurs, 10 AM – 7 PM
Wed, Fri, Sat, 10 AM - 5:30 PM
Sun and Mon, Closed

---

e: 3/5/2020 Time: 3:46:48 PM

ms checked out this session: 1

---

e: Getting real about getting older : c
code: 33021032178227
Date: 03/26/20

Page 1 of 1

... where anything is possible.

die shortly thereafter. Over the years, however, life expectancies have increased so much that most women live nearly a third of their lives post-menopause. In essence, these years mark a new beginning, a new freedom. Without the burden of reproductive responsibilities, women can experience new opportunities to grow and achieve. We resist the invisibility that losing our sexual identity can mean, but accepting these physical changes and acknowledging their benefits can make the journey so much easier.

> *I was traveling last summer. On my own. It was an incredible experience. I didn't worry about being accosted or fending off unwanted advances. I felt such freedom. Of course, I avoided the sleazier parts of the city and didn't stay out late, but I came and went as I pleased and had a blast. The only concern I had was pickpockets in Rome.*
>
> —Eighty-one-year-old world traveler

So, do we really become invisible as we age, or are we now just wise enough to understand that people really don't pay much attention to anyone else, regardless of how old they are? Everyone is essentially self-absorbed, worrying and fretting about themselves. There's a saying: "You wouldn't worry about what people thought of you if you knew how seldom they did."*

As we age, most of us finally become less egocentric and realize we are not on center stage and probably never were anyway. We recognize that most people aren't really thinking or talking about us and, like us, are just trying to take care of themselves. Ann Landers summed this up well: "At age 10, we worry about what others think of us, at age 40, we don't care what they think of us, and at age 60, we discover they haven't *been* thinking about us!"[13] That knowledge can be liberating, as we see that we now can live our lives with fewer constraints about how we *should* behave or be. Getting older doesn't have to mean fading from view.

Our respondents' experiences of feeling invisible, and their reactions to the often painful situations they found themselves in, speak volumes about the resilience of the human spirit.

---

*   Attributed to various individuals.

Chapter 3

AM I STILL ME?

"A rose by any other name would smell as sweet."

—WILLIAM SHAKESPEARE

Did you read *Alice's Adventures in Wonderland* as a child? One of our favorite conversations in the book occurs when Caterpillar is sitting on the mushroom and says to Alice, "Who...are...*you*?" Alice is a bit stunned and not sure how to respond. "I—I hardly know, sir, just at present," she replies. "At least I know who I *was* when I got up this morning, but I think I must have been changed several times since then."

Alice is frequently puzzled about who she is or is becoming. Earlier in the book, she says to herself, "I wonder if I've been changed in the night? Let me think. Was I the same when I got up this morning? I almost think I can remember feeling a little different. But if I'm not the same, the next question is, Who in the world am I?"

Many aging adults feel a lot like Alice. We hardly know who we are. Like Alice, we seem to have changed so much that we hardly recognize ourselves. It may be too strong to say we're having an identity crisis, but maybe that's just how we *should* view it.

So, who *are* we? We know who we *were* (moms, managers, dads, kids' coaches, factory workers, salespeople), but who are we *now*? Now that we're retired and our identity isn't defined by what we did or who we were caring for, how do we define who we are? Here's what one of our respondents had to say:

I know what I used to be... I used to be CEO of a major Fortune 500 company. I used to have a corner office in the biggest high-rise in town. I'm just not exactly sure what I am now. I find I keep defining myself by what I was because I don't know what I am.

—Seventy-two-year-old former corner-office guy

To adjust successfully to older age, as to all developmental stages, you have to define yourself by who you *are*, not by who you *were,* whether you were a CEO, a farmer, a salesperson, a stay-at-home mom, or a teacher. Who are you *now*? If you don't know, it's time to find out.

— YOU'RE MORE THAN YOUR WRINKLES —

Your outward appearance affects how others label or perceive you. The pigeon thinks Alice is a serpent because of her long neck. Similarly, you may be wrinkled, you may stoop a bit as you walk, and your pace may have slowed; in other words, you may be showing signs of aging. While others may think of you this way, your inner self—your image of who you are—may not have changed for decades.

Are other people's labels meaningful in helping to define us? Maybe so. Like the woman quoted below, the first time we recognize we are changing may occur when those around us see us as an older person, even before we do.

I took a trip overseas this past year. I've been schlep-ping my bags all over the world by myself for years, given my profession included a lot of international travel. I haven't traveled alone for some time, so it struck me as odd that many people were offering to help me move my bags onto the transfer belt as I went through TSA. "May I help you place that bag in the overhead bin?" asked the kind gentleman sitting next to me on the plane. People step aside, allowing me to move ahead of them; pause briefly to show deference to me. I guess I kinda liked it, but it also made me realize that I am different now. I am elderly. I hate the term, but even though I don't feel it, others must see it.

—Seventy-year-old world-traveling woman

For most of us, it's not just that our sense of who we are has changed, but that we've also changed in the eyes of those around us. We're not the same people we were ten or twenty years ago, and that can be a bit scary for the people in our lives. Sometimes the changes they see in us can make them realize that they, too, are getting older and their identities are changing. Parents may no longer be the emotional, financial, and helpful safety net they once were, and the adult children may sense that they will soon have to be the *strong* ones. This is difficult for both older parents and their adult children. Just as an uncomfortable, sometimes scary, shift in identity is happening in the older adults, it's happening simultaneously in the adult children, and they may not like it. They may even actively resist it by trying to ignore the noticeable changes.

One of the men we interviewed didn't think of himself as old and wanted to ignore the label.

Aging is all about labels, I think. We need to put a label on everything. And labels come with instructions. What would happen if you ignored the labels and the instructions and just used that new gizmo the way you want? Is the world going to come to a screeching halt just because you chose not to play by the rules? My guess is no. In fact, nobody really cares at all what you do. That's liberating. So, forget about the label of your age and the proper behavior that comes with that age. Nobody's watching, and even if they are, so what?

—Seventy-four-year-old label ignorer

Our peers are likely to recognize that if we look older, they must look older, too, forcing some to redefine who they are in their own eyes, as well as in those of their contemporaries.

I went to my fifty-year college fraternity reunion this year. I hadn't seen most of these guys for years. What a shock. They looked old. Made me realize I must look old too.

—Seventy-three-year-old frat boy

I thought I looked pretty good for seventy-eight. I never really thought that I was that old. I know some people, maybe most people, might think this is old, but I'm in pretty good shape. I still play tennis and move around pretty good. Want a real shocker? Go to your sixtieth high school class reunion. First you recognize that a few people are missing (they've died, are in the hospital, or couldn't get out of bed to come). They are wrinkled up like prunes. Everyone kept telling me that I had really changed. Had they looked in the mirror lately?

—Seventy-eight-year-old reunion guy

Many of our survey respondents told us that they saw themselves as separate from their bodies. They didn't recognize the person they saw in the mirror or in the window as they were walking down the street. They were often caught by surprise and dismay and would ask themselves, "Who is that person looking back at me?" They were alienated and estranged from the person they saw in the mirror, puzzled by who that person was, and often refused to admit that the visible changes were really occurring and that this new body in the mirror was *really* theirs. One respondent noted:

I remember getting up one morning. I realized I'd been avoiding looking in the mirror these days. But this morning, for some reason, that full-length mirror was beckoning for my attention. As I was getting dressed, with few clothes on at this point, I was reminded of those comedians who mimic someone, as if they are the true reflection in the mirror. They imitate every movement of the other person—it is often very humorous. If the person's arm goes up, they simulate the action, if the person turns his or her head, they are in sync with that movement. Well…that's exactly what I thought was happening; when I turned around, that person in the mirror turned around too. When I lifted my arm to examine my body more closely, the person in the mirror did the same thing—the only thing was, it wasn't quite as humorous as when I had watched it on television. There was a person in my mirror, one I didn't fully recognize, but yet a person who looked a lot like me, but…she had unbelievably crinkly skin—not just her arms, but all over her body. I remember my mouth actually opening and dropping in sheer disbelief! I, of course, knew I had some wrinkles, but this was shocking. My arms and legs just didn't seem to be mine—where did mine go? And just when did this happen? That was a turnaround day for me—the first day that I really knew I was old.

—Seventy-two-year-old in disbelief

While this detachment from our bodies may seem harmless and something we can deal with, it can delay us from forming appropriate new identities as we age. Psychologists might call this a defense mechanism. They might also call it a poor one.

Just as adolescents often feel uncomfortable about their bodies, so do older people. That is because, as author and psychotherapist Kristi Pikiewicz claims, we think of our bodies as *home*. Because so many changes are happening to them physically, both adolescents and older people feel they have lost their *home*.[14] Other than in adolescence, we undergo no more drastic changes in our physical bodies than those that occur after age sixty-five. As in adolescence, adapting to those changes can be challenging indeed.

As your outward appearance changes, your first instinct may be to resist what is happening to you physically. On one hand, you may develop a defensive posture in an attempt to maintain the status quo. On the other hand, you may be more like this respondent, who accepted her physical changes with humor and pride. Identifying and understanding your resistance to all the changes you're experiencing will help you adapt and to grasp that a redefinition of who you are is necessary.

I've earned every line in this face of mine. I've got friends who are proud of their smooth complexions. More power to them. I think they show about as much life experience in those faces as a two-year-old. And what's the point? Does it really matter if I show up at my funeral with smooth skin or a wrinkled hide? Won't make any difference to me. Honestly, if they'd had sunblock when I was a kid, I probably would have used it, but they didn't. So, this is what I look like. Those lines around my eyes? Some come from laughter, some come from worry, but erasing them won't erase the experiences that caused them. They are part of me. I like to look at a person whose face shows a life well lived, not a life wasted in the shade. I find the former infinitely more interesting.

—Seventy-four-year-old life-well-lived woman

There's another scene in *Alice's Adventures in Wonderland* that may remind you of situations you've been in. While Alice is in the Looking Glass woods, she can't remember her name. She becomes frightened by her lapse of memory. You may have that same sense of frustration and fear when you can't remember something. Like Alice, most of us finally remember what it is we were trying to think of, but there's still frustration, and we can become frightened. Yes, you are getting older, and a senior moment is a reminder.

As with all the changes you'll experience as you get older, senior moments may seem significant. While they can be frightening, such lapses in memory don't need to take on too great an importance. Some people, for example, can forget a few things and laugh it off, while others, having the same loss of memory, can convince themselves they have a serious disease, such as Alzheimer's. It's too easy to fall into the trap of letting a relatively minor change start a downward spiral of expectations about who you are now and what your life will be like in the future.

☞ REALITY CHECK

Consider some of these questions as you try to figure out just who you are *now*.

1. How do people react to you now that you look older?

2. How does this make you feel? How do you respond?

3. What age do you think of yourself? How about after you look in a mirror?

4. What experiences have affected your perceptions?

5. Have you had *senior moments*? How did you react to them?

6. What might these *senior moments* say about your attitudes toward aging?

7. What other changes that you're experiencing have also been frightening?

SO, WHO ARE YOU ANYWAY?

Have you ever tried to answer the question "Who am I?" It's a difficult question to answer, isn't it? Go ahead, take a moment, and try to answer the question. What did you come up with?

Here's how two of our respondents replied:

I'm a seventy-year-old man. I am treading water and happy to be treading water. The other choice is that I would be dead!
—Seventy-year-old water-treading man

It was daylight savings day. One more hour to sleep in, well, maybe one more hour to lay awake in the morning, assess what my day might look like. I'm sixty-six years old today. I try to think about whether I ever thought about being sixty-six. If I did, I bet I thought it would be more perfect than this. With my extra hour today, I find myself wishing things were different—that my husband was more loving, complimentary, and adoring, like all of the fairytale stories I read to my granddaughter; that my kids were more attentive and doting, my grandkids calling me every day, wishing I was with them. I wish I had been more successful, made a real mark on the world. Helped solve world peace, fed the hungry, and cared for the sick. I sulk and I drown in my disappointment and flawed expectations. And I wonder, did I ever think about being sixty-six and what it would be like? Who I'd be? In fact, who am I? I...just...don't...know.

—Sixty-six-year-old flawed-expectations woman

Scholars tell us that as we age, we need to have a clear sense of our identity, because, like a compass, it guides us through the travels of our lives.[15] It allows us to understand our life experiences and gives us a sense of self. Our individual experiences are also important in shaping our sense of self.

Having a strong and clear sense of self can help us navigate the challenges of growing older and help ensure healthy adaptation to the latter years of our lives. The trick is to strike a balance between our sense of who we've been and who we are becoming. Having a healthy self-perception isn't all it takes to develop a healthy identity. How and where we fit into our social settings and social groups (family, friends, work, community) are also extremely important.

Like most people, we can't help but unconsciously classify and compare ourselves to others. After all, a huge part of our identity is related to our social environment and how we measure up. And therein may lie a problem. It seems that, as we age, our most significant *other* may be our former self—who we *used* to be. And often we feel as if we don't measure up. It's very hard for some of us to let go of our former identities. Wasn't it just yesterday that people were calling us for help with one thing or another? Are there as many such requests recently?

As we discussed in previous chapters, it's part of the human developmental process to move from one stage to the next. Those of us who adapt best are constantly adjusting to our new stages of life physically, socially, and emotionally.

Our identity—how we live, what we do, the decisions we make—plays a significant role in shaping our lives at each stage of our development. We are pretty clear about what we need to do at each of the earlier stages to be prepared for the next, yet, as should be clearer now, many of us are woefully unprepared for getting older.

Our identities are not fixed in stone but change across major life transitions. Research suggests that having multiple roles is associated with better health and psychological well-being.[16] Simply put, the more we do, the more people we interact with, the better off we are. Participation in the broader community is likely to lead to strong role identity, which is beneficial for both our health and the health of our overall community.

☞ REALITY CHECK

What have you been doing to maintain some of the multiple roles you had when you were younger? Answering these specific questions may help you answer this broader one.

1. Are you involved in your community? What additional activities would you consider doing?

2. Do you volunteer? Would you like to?

3. Do you spend time in nature? There are many ways to do this, even if it's just sitting under a tree reading.

4. Do you give yourself time to relax? You've earned it.

5. How about time for quiet reflection? How much such time do you give yourself?

6. What about your spiritual life (e.g., attending church, meditating, being part of or starting a study group, reading books on spiritual topics)?

——— **CARVING OUT A NEW IDENTITY** ———

You may have already realized that how you feel has less to do with your chronological age and more to do with your health and other factors. You've probably met people who felt young at seventy and others twenty years younger who seemed old and felt old. What's important is how old we *feel*, not how old we *are*.

Our age identity is totally subjective and can be unrelated to how old we actually are. Age identity can be affected, however, by objective changes related to our life experiences. These changes can include stress, physical health, and mental well-being.

Those of us with significant health problems generally feel older than those without. Surely, illnesses such as cancer and heart disease are flashing banners reminding us of our vulnerability and mortality and, in some cases, of the short time we have left. Yet many of us know someone who has serious health problems and who continues to be happy, kind, and generous of spirit. Those of us who have less stress, fewer illnesses, and less conflict in our lives have a younger age identity, for sure.

The lesson here seems to be that while we can't do anything about our chronological age, there are things we *can* do to change our subjective age identity—how we feel as we get older. Even if we have a serious illness, we can control how we adapt to the change in our health and its effects on us. Reminding ourselves of the countless numbers of people who continue to make the most of their lives despite their illnesses may help. Those who come back from combat as paraplegics are a good example. Many come home and continue to live full lives, learning new skills, furthering their education, and engaging in activities that meld with their physical situation. They can be inspiring examples of how to maneuver through life. The key is to accept new situations and circumstances and immediately work to find ways to adapt to them physically and psychologically.

As we've seen, there are a number of similarities between old age and adolescence. Author and therapist Pikiewicz claims that, like adolescents, older people are often clearer about the identity they *don't* want than the one they do. In both stages, the outside world often challenges our abilities to be who we thought we were, as we struggle to find a new identity that better suits our new developmental stage.

Like adolescence, there is likely a conflicting sense of self as we get older, as this respondent noted:

I sometimes have trouble identifying with this new "me." What happened to the real "me"? Who is this person looking back at me in the mirror? I felt so much more comfortable

with the old me. This new body, mind, spirit, sometimes
just doesn't fit right.

—Seventy-seven-year-old looking-in-the-mirror gal

There are opportunities, however, to create a new identity. One of our respondents did a pretty good job of doing just that.

I can hardly remember the person who was a success-
ful consultant all her life, consulting with CEOs of major
Fortune 500 corporations. Sometimes, I'm asked to submit
my bio somewhere and I can't even believe that person was
me. Guess I've done a good job of creating a new identity as
I age. I don't even know that person anymore.

—Seventy-five-year-old former consultant

One way to help form a new identity is to pursue hobbies and interests you may never have had time for. Maybe you've always wanted to learn Italian or play the flute or tennis or golf. Embracing any or all of these activities can help you carve a new identity that you may truly enjoy while keeping you young in spirit and engaged in the world around you.

Just because our bodies have changed doesn't mean we aren't capable of doing some awesome things. Remember, John Glenn went into space at age seventy-seven and was the oldest person to do so. While we may not all be capable of his achievements late in life, we can all still make a difference.

Becoming elderly often takes us by surprise. Unlike other stages of life, we have done little to prepare for this one. It's clear with other stages of our life that we literally take on a new identity—of spouse or partner, parent, new brand manager, shift supervisor, doctor, lawyer, factory worker. Most of us, however, are not aware that we have a new identity or need to create one as we become older.

We began this chapter by talking about *Alice's Adventures in Wonderland*. Like many of us, Alice sometimes doesn't really know who she is and is puzzled by it. She is worried about her own power and autonomy. We tend to be worried, too, as we get older.

Like Alice, you can keep searching. When that search is effective, you will meet the new person you have become. When you do, we hope the new person you find is wiser, mentally stronger, and, of course, kinder.

☞ REALITY CHECK

You may have to spend some time reacquainting yourself with your new body, new experiences, and new self. Keep searching until you find an identity and environment that fits and feels right. Answering the following questions may help:

1. Who are you now? How has your identity changed now that you're older? This information has to be assimilated into what you already know about yourself. You need to change the idea of who you are to create an identity you're comfortable with. Don't settle on an identity until you find one that fits just right.

2. Now use this information to help you reframe not only who you are but who you want to be.

3. Then think about how to use the valuable time you have remaining.

Chapter 4

BATTLE OF THE SEXES

"Nobody will ever win the battle of the sexes.
There is too much fraternizing with the enemy."

—HENRY KISSINGER

Remember when Billy Jean King beat Bobby Riggs in that famous tennis match in the 1970s? Many thought it was a sign of things to come. Women would finally be seen as men's equals in the workplace, in the home, and on the political scene…but not so fast. Our generation may think the battle of the sexes began with Billy Jean and Bobby, but it's a battle that has been going on since the beginning of time, especially as it relates to aging.

THE AGING PROCESS IS DIFFERENT FOR MEN AND WOMEN

Psychologists tell us that men and women do age differently, and our respondents agree. For sure, young girls develop physically much more quickly than do young boys, but it is less clear how or why women age more quickly than men.

How people age is determined in large part by lifestyle decisions over which they have a great deal of control, such as whether they're smokers or heavy drinkers, as well as what they eat and how much they exercise. Men and women are remarkably alike in the effects of lifestyle decisions on the aging process, and it's no secret that maintaining a healthy lifestyle helps both men and women age well. Level of education, working conditions, and basic health care also influence aging, as do the culture you're born into, and, of course, your gene pool.

On average, women outlive men. Women live an average of 81.2 years, while men live an average of 76.3 years.[17] There's good news for men, however; this gap seems to be narrowing. According to the 2010 census, the percentage of men in the United States over the age of sixty-five has been increasing at a significantly faster rate than for women for the first time since data have been collected. Among men in the oldest age group (between eighty-five and ninety-four) the increase was 46.5 percent, versus 22.9 percent for women. The highest ratio of women to men, however, is still in our later years.

There is much debate about why women generally outlive men. Some researchers point to genetic differences, and others to the incidence of heart disease, cancer, and other diseases that have higher fatality rates in men than in women. Finally, men, as a group, engage in riskier behaviors, which, of course, affects the statistics.[18]

While scientists offer several explanations for why women live longer, our female respondents came up with another idea: women can't get the men in their lives to go to the doctor. They just might be right!

I honestly don't understand my husband. He simply refuses to go to the doctor about anything. He says they won't be able to do anything about his arthritis, and I told him he's right. If he won't do anything to help himself, such as making an appointment to find out what can be done, nothing will get done. In the meantime, he's in pain. I can see it in his eyes, and I definitely can tell he's hurting because he's so grumpy. I'm at my wit's end.

—Seventy-five-year-old fed-up wife

My brother had this black mole on his forehead. He used to joke about it until one day, he went to the doctor for a blood pressure check. Turned out the black mole was a melanoma and he'd waited too long. They took it off, but he had to go the chemo route and he was so sick. He didn't get better. I wish I'd been more insistent, but I kept thinking he knew what he was doing. He didn't. I think he was waiting for somebody to give him some sort of permission to go get it looked at so he didn't appear to be foolish.

—Seventy-year-old shoulda-been-a-nag sister

Yes, I'm a first-class nag. I admit it. And it's a damn good thing I am, or my husband would be pushing up daisies. That pain in his left shoulder worried me. He was short of breath, too, so I did the only thing I could think of. I called the doctor's office and made an appointment. Then, I asked him if he wanted to go to the store with me, and when he got in the car, I drove straight to the doctor's office, turned off the car and asked him if he wanted to go inside, or would he rather go inside the funeral home and sign the papers. He grumbled, but he went in. He needed a double bypass and I didn't even tell him, "I told you so." He's still around and I'm glad.

—Seventy-six-year-old glad-she's-a-nag wife

Are you familiar with the book *Men Are from Mars, Women Are from Venus*? Many of our female respondents would agree that men are definitely from Mars when it comes to caring for themselves.

They say ignorance is bliss, and, if it's true, my spouse is the most blissful person on the planet. He just seems to assume everything will just happen without any work on his part. Of course, I guess he's right. He's got me. I guess it's my job to take care of him. I've been doing it for nearly fifty years now, and if he's clueless about what to do, I guess it's my fault as much as his. Do modern wives still have to take care of their spouse's health?

—Seventy-eight-year-old not-so-blissful wife

My wife spends all her time at the doctor's office. If she's not going to the skin doctor to have a practically invisible spot frozen off her cheek, she's at the foot doctor complaining about her bunions. I think she goes a little overboard on this doctor thing.

—Seventy-year-old not-going-overboard husband

☞ REALITY CHECK

Maybe our respondents are on to something. Maybe women do pay better attention to their health and address medical concerns a lot sooner than men do. Maybe they're better educated in how to prevent illnesses and how to identify problems when they do arise. And just maybe this is one of the reasons why women live longer than men.

1. If you're one of those people who won't go to the doctor until you're at death's door, or if you're living with someone like this, what are the excuses for not going? What do you think is causing the resistance?

2. If you're the "nag," what new approach might you consider using to get this person to the doctor? How about stories of people who overlooked warning signals? Are there changes in your spouse that you're concerned about? Are there friends or other family members who might be better at convincing this person to change his or her behavior?

3. There's always room for improvement when it comes to our diets, drinking habits, and exercise regimens. What changes could you make with your spouse that would encourage both of you to improve your habits?

——— GENDER-RELATED DISEASES ———
ARE NO LAUGHING MATTER

The differences between men and women have been fodder for comedians forever, but as with most humor, there's some truth behind the jokes. There really are differences, at least in the likelihood of getting certain diseases, and consequently, in having to care for a spouse or family member with one of these diseases. Men are 1.5 times more likely to develop Parkinson's disease, for instance, and women are twice as likely as men to get Alzheimer's. As some of our respondents explained, compassion and patience are key if you're a caregiver, and they're not always easy to draw upon.

My wife has Alzheimer's. It came on slowly, as it often does, but it seems to be progressing rapidly. I used to get impatient with her. Now I wish I'd understood what was happening. You never know until it's too late. Some days she recognizes me, and that's a good day. I'd give anything to have a second chance at this. I'd do it right. At least, I like to think I would.
—Eighty-two-year-old wishes-he-could-do-it-better guy

I'd promised my mother I'd never put her in a convalescent hospital, and at the time, I was convinced I could keep that promise. But her dementia got worse, and she began to wander. I was still working, and finding someone to stay with her while I was gone became harder and harder. I tried to honor my promise, but I couldn't. She's safe in the memory care facility, but I think sometimes, when her mind clears, she remembers what she asked me.

—Sixty-five-year-old couldn't-keep-his-promise son

My wife has Parkinson's and has trouble with her balance. She's tired a lot and needs help with some things. Sometimes, it's tough to keep smiling when I help her. I worry about what will happen if I go first. I worry about the finances and what it will cost to keep her at home.

—Eighty-one-year-old worrying husband

Not all of our experiences with gender and illness are serious. Sometimes, they're just annoying or puzzling. Regardless of age, sometimes we just have difficulty understanding those we care about, and this is reflected in our everyday language:

"Are you nuts?"

"Are you out of your mind?"

"What was he thinking?"

"How could she do/say that?"

"Is he *crazy*?"

───── WHO AGES BETTER? ─────

Some women feel that men have the advantage when it comes to aging because they undergo fewer noticeable negative physical changes. As just one example, haven't we all experienced or at least observed women having hot flashes or shared the experience with a friend? It's hard to miss.

Menopause? Oh, honey, I could tell you stories. I like to think of myself as my very own central heating unit. If there's ever a power outage, I can just have my family gather around me while I give off radiant heat and warm up the room. I'll be first on everybody's go-to list. I was still working, and it was miserable. I would turn red as a beet. I could literally feel it starting at my neck and moving up. If I was giving a presentation, it was obvious to everybody in the room what was happening. It's got to be number one on any woman's list of most embarrassing situations.

—Sixty-five-year-old still heat-'em-up gal

Some of our women respondents resented that men seem to age better than they did. Men's hair turns a distinguished-looking gray, yet the same hair color in women is often thought to look washed out and unattractive. Older men are often considered handsome well into their later years, while older women spend a lot of time and money trying to look younger than their age: coloring their hair, using cosmetics, and maybe trying Botox injections or plastic surgery.

Is there anything more pathetic than a woman who should be old enough to know better trying to look like a teeny bopper or whatever they call those young girls today? It's ridiculous. They either need new glasses, a full-length mirror, or a brain transplant. They aren't fooling anybody.

—Seventy-seven-year-old with-a-full-length-mirror gal

One area in which women win hands down is they're less likely to go bald. They may lose some hair and the texture may change, but they don't seem to develop those shiny pates the way some men do. No, women don't have to worry as much as their male counterparts about receding hairlines or going bald, but that's not to say that they don't notice differences.

My hair has definitely gotten thinner. It never was all that thick to begin with, and now it's downright wispy. Also, my eyebrows seem to have disappeared for the most part. I wonder where they went? At least I don't have to shave my legs or underarms anymore, and that's good. Hair is

disappearing from everywhere it should be and showing up
where it shouldn't be.

    —Seventy-two-year-old still-got-some-hair gal

There's some scientific basis for our perceptions about the physical differences in patterns of aging: men really do get fewer wrinkles. There are a few reasons for this, including male testosterone and the fact that men have thicker skin.[19] This isn't to say that they're better able to tolerate insults or teasing, but it does mean that their age may be less visible on their faces. Some women in our study didn't think this was fair.

We'll be driving in the car and sometimes my husband
will reach over and touch my cheek. From time to time he
just seems to stare at my face. He's not being affectionate.
He seems to be feeling the wrinkle or comparing me to the
way I used to look. It bothers me. I look older than he does.
    —Seventy-one-year-old wrinkled-in-the-
    passenger-seat gal

Women also typically gain weight as they age and have more trouble taking it off than when they were younger. We've all heard comments like these:

I lost twenty pounds for my big round-the-world trip celebrating my retirement. And by the time I'd gotten halfway around the globe, I'd put ten back on. It's always been harder for me to lose weight than my husband, but now that I'm older it's more difficult than ever. I give up. In my next life, I'm going to be slim. My husband gives up one beer a day and he drops five pounds overnight. Go figure!

—Sixty-six-year-old giving-up-on-losing gal

I have three wardrobes. Fat, fatter, and time to go back to Weight Watchers. I think I'm on the third time through each of them.

—Seventy-year-old third-time-around gal

An expanding midsection can be a problem for men too. Like women, their metabolism changes in their later years, and their testosterone levels drop.

My brother-in-law, that old goat, he thinks he's still sexy. He's got a belly and hasn't seen his toes in years. Why do men think like that? He still tries to get the girls to look at him. They look at him all right. If looks could kill!

—Seventy-eight-year-old goat's sister-in-law

Finally, there's the question of whether the size of men's and women's brains change as they get older. Aging includes many physical, biological, chemical, and psychological changes, so it is no surprise that aging also affects brain size. Most scientists agree that our brains decrease in size as we age. Factors such as high blood pressure, weight gain, and especially neuronal cell death are contributing factors to the decline in the size of older adults' brains. For the most part, however, science is still unclear on what causes this decline in brain size.[20]

Generally speaking, women's brains are smaller than men's.[21] But, as women often like to remind men, size doesn't matter. Scientists agree that when it comes to our brains, it's true. Size really doesn't matter; otherwise, animals with very large brains might rule the world (think elephants or whales). The bottom line is that the data relating to the differences between male and female brains as they age remains ambiguous at best. One thing scientists do seem confident about, however, is that whether you're male or female, your brain becomes smaller as you get older. Let's just leave this discussion now, shall we?

☞ REALITY CHECK

Here are some questions to ponder as you think about the differences between men and women in their later years.

1. What, if any, perceptions have you bought into about being an older man or woman? Are any of these perceptions based in truth? If not, why do you think they're perpetuated in the media or even in casual conversation?

2. Who do you know who has aged successfully? Are they doing anything that you might incorporate into your own life?

3. There's no way to avoid aging, but what changes might you make to age more gracefully and make your life more interesting, engaging, or more fun?

— IS THERE A BATTLE IN THE BEDROOM? —

Regardless of their age, men are much more sexually driven than are women. Even after age sixty, men fantasize about sex much more than women.[22] This is not likely to come as a surprise to most women.

The women in our study told us they were always more interested in the quality, not the quantity, of the sex; and that's borne out by scientific studies. Our respondents corroborated another finding, which is that sexual satisfaction among women increases with age. In one study of older, sexually active women, two-thirds reported that they were moderately or very satisfied with their sex lives. Older men are generally as satisfied or even more satisfied as well, and for many older people, sex in their sixties is better than ever. They often have more time and fewer distractions, and getting older often means becoming more comfortable in your skin.

Sex is much easier now. I think the pressure's off. We're comfortable with each other, and we're used to each other. It's a good feeling.

—Sixty-seven-year-old feeling-good gal

Other respondents indicated that they had never been that interested in sex—at any age.

My mother always said that women need a reason to have sex. Men just need a place. Well, I think it's true, and I don't have much of a reason anymore. Sex never interested me all that much, and I'm fine without it.

—Seventy-year-old listening-to-her-mom gal

Finally, for some of our respondents, health problems had forced them to put sex on the back burner.

After my prostate surgery, sex was too difficult. I still think about sex from time to time, but it's a chapter closed. I don't think my wife minds. At least she doesn't say anything. But we never talked about sex, so I don't really know what she thinks.

—Seventy-one-year-old still-thinking-about-it guy

OUR COPING STRATEGIES ARE DIFFERENT TOO

Outwardly, men may appear to age more comfortably than women do, but research suggests that aging is generally more difficult for men than for women.[23] It seems that, over time, women have developed ways to cope more appropriately with change, depression, stress, and other common experiences of old age.

Women may appear older earlier than men, but perhaps because they tend to live longer than men do, they ultimately have longer to figure out how to cope with the changes that aging brings. It's not that aging is easier for women; in many ways it's more difficult, given the differences in how society perceives older men and women. Still, it's no secret that women, especially older women, have learned to adapt and live within more restrictive boundaries that society has established for them. Women are often more willing to share their challenges with friends and work together to find ways to cope, whether by making new friends, trying new activities, or seeking professional help. Men struggle more with their loss of strength, loss of professional identity, and greater isolation in the community.

I used to put in a full day's work and then come home and work in the yard or my shop. Now, after three or four hours of just puttering around, I'm tired. It's not that I can't do the work, it's just that I don't have the stamina I used to.

—Seventy-one-year-old puttering-around guy

I take a nap every afternoon. Not for very long, maybe twenty minutes or so, but it restores my energy. My wife laughs at me, but she falls asleep in her chair. At least I've got sense enough to go stretch out so I don't get a kink in my neck.

—Seventy-seven-year-old no-kink-in-the-neck guy

Most of the people in our study thought men and women become more *alike,* not more *different,* as we grow older. We agree. Our respondents noted that chores around the house were often no longer gender-determined. Both men and women cooked, shopped for groceries, washed dishes, and worked together on the outside chores. Women commented that the older men in their lives had become more sensitive and often teared up on special occasions or at movies, when that would never have happened when they were younger. And, in another example of busting open gender stereotypes, women told us how they'd been forced, or had chosen, to learn more about their family finances and, in many cases, had become the chief financial officers of their homes.

There's no doubt that aging can be difficult for both men and women, but evidence suggests that, despite sagging skin and expanding waistlines, older people are happier than younger ones.[24] This may be because older adults are more content with what they have and are often finally better able to shrug off insignificant annoyances. In other words, they feel they are being rewarded for their years of experience.

I remember that line, "Grow old along with me, the best is yet to be." I don't know if this is the best, but we're still together after fifty years, and I think I made a good choice. Growing older has its ups and downs for both men and women for sure, but it is a whole lot easier when you share the journey with someone else you care for, be it your spouse, partner, or significant other.

—Seventy-eight-year-old
thinks-she-made-a-good-choice gal

So, what about the battle of the sexes? Our generation hasn't solved all of its gender issues, but our respondents agree that the differences between men and women are becoming less significant and less constraining. Whether you're nine or ninety, male or female, the ideas about gender that define how you should look, act, and think are a lot more fluid than they used to be, and our generation has had a lot to do with the positive changes that have occurred.

Chapter 5

THE PARENT–ADULT CHILD RELATIONSHIP

Can We Do Better?

"There is no friendship, no love, like that of the parent for the child."

—HENRY WARD BEECHER

The parent–adult child relationship is often one of the longest-lasting, most intense relationships we have in our lifetimes. It's important for the relationship to remain healthy over our lifespan, because a positive bond can have a huge impact on each party's health and well-being and can be a tremendous source of social, psychological, and physical support. It's also just really fun to enjoy our relationships with our grown children.

The years when we are raising our children in our homes

are a relatively short period of time. If we're fortunate to live long enough, we're likely to spend far more years as parents of children eighteen years and older. The relationship we have with these children can be enormously fulfilling and rewarding, or it can be fraught with tension and ambivalence. This chapter provides some insights into this important relationship and suggests ways to make it one of the most valued we will ever experience.

FACE IT, IT'S A ONE-WAY STREET

Many of our respondents told us that their relationship with their adult children sometimes feels like a one-way street. This shouldn't come as a surprise, since most parents love their children way more than their children love them. That's the layperson's way of explaining what psychologists call the *developmental stake hypothesis*: parents are more emotionally invested in their children than their children are in them.[25] This disparity occurs across the lifespan. It's not just our adult children whom we love more than they love us; rather, it's our children at all ages. From toddlers to teenagers to adults, our children may love us very deeply, but research and theory support the notion that the strongest feelings are from the parent to the child. You have most likely experienced this in your own relationships with your children, and understanding this phenomenon, *really* understanding it, might have eliminated a lot of tension. This respondent seems to understand it well:

> *My daughter called me one day in tears. She told me that her son [my grandson] asked her not to come to the baseball game that he was going to after school. "Just come afterward and pick me up," he said. "I'll meet you in the parking lot around five o'clock." She told me that she realized he had a life without her that didn't include her—that he now wanted to do lots of "stuff" without her. I didn't say it, but I wanted to say, "Buckle up." This is just the beginning of being left out of their lives, of their growing away from you. It's not a bad thing. That's how it's supposed to be.*
>
> —Seventy-one-year-old buckled-up grandma

Maybe a one-way street isn't so bad after all. One-way streets have higher traffic flow, because drivers don't have to steer clear of oncoming traffic, and there's less congestion; as such, they can serve a very useful purpose. Seeing our relationships with our adult children as one-sided, or at least lopsided, is useful as well. This seventy-two-year-old dad observed:

Some of my friends complain that their adult kids don't have time for them. They are busy with their own children, ballgames, plays; they have lots of stuff going on. Not me. I'm proud of them for doing exactly what they should be doing!

—Seventy-two-year-old proud dad

Parents of all ages tend to expect and want more out of their relationships with their children than is developmentally possible for the children to provide. Depending on the developmental stage of your children, for instance, whether they are teenagers or older adults, you and they may have different needs in the relationship. As noted by respondents in our surveys and interviews, this disparity can lead to tension. For the most part, parents want to be more involved with their adult children as the children are moving on with their own independent lives. Again, understanding this, *really* understanding it, can make you a better parent at every stage of your life and your children's lives, especially as they become adults with families of their own. This seventy-four-year-old grandma gets it:

I miss my kids so much. I want to be around them more, yet I know they have vibrant lives of their own and I'm not part of most of it. I didn't have my parents as part of our lives in many ways, so what makes me think I should be involved in everything they do? I realize it isn't that I think I "should" be, I just "want" to be. Then, I get out of my own ego and realize what a wonderful job of parenting they are doing. I just need to keep remembering that and get on with my own life.

—Seventy-four-year-old

getting-on-with-her-own-life grandma

☞ REALITY CHECK

These tips may help you come to terms with the fact that your attachment to your children will always be stronger than their attachment to you.

1. Get really clear on the fact that your children may love you but there is *no* way they can love you in the same way you love them.

2. Understand that, consequently, in every inter-action, you have more to gain and more to lose. If your children have children of their own, someday they will become immensely aware of this difference.

3. As the older parents quoted above recognize,
    it's best to accept this difference in needs. It's
    one of those things we simply can't change.

Now that we've established the developmental stake
hypothesis and realize that it's inevitable that you will
love your children at every age of their lives more than
they'll love you, how can you achieve a relationship
with them as adults that is healthy and loving even if
tensions may occur?

BE CAREFUL ABOUT OFFERING UNSOLICITED ADVICE

Even the parents we interviewed who had good relationships
with their adult children sometimes experienced tension with
them. Research has shown that one of the biggest causes of this
tension between parents and children is offering unsolicited
advice. Accepting what another person may think of as helpful
feedback is never easy, whether the person giving the advice is
an aging parent, a boss, or a friend.

Our respondents noted that they experienced times when
they just couldn't resist telling their adult children what they
were certain was a better way to deal with their children, to
relate to their spouse, to...well, you get the picture. Most of

us are simply trying to make our children's lives better. We did the same thing by giving advice when they were young. Regardless of their age, we should all think twice before handing out *expert* unsolicited advice. Three respondents reflected on advice-giving this way:

In one of my most uncomfortable conversations with my daughter-in-law, she requested that I should stop giving her advice about how to raise her kids because she was married to one of mine and he still needed quite a bit of work too.

—Sixty-eight-year-old uncomfortable grandmother

I'm sure you've often heard that grandparents have to keep their mouths shut…be careful to not upset the apple cart or you won't get invited to events and you won't get to see the grandkids as much as you would like. I always thought that was just kind of a joke. It's not; it's for real. It's just one more example of how we are losing control over our lives. Little by little, one more thing each month and year that we don't have complete control over. I hate to use the word "power," but I guess that's what it is. We are losing more and more power over our lives every day.

—Seventy-seven-year-old losing-control grandfather

My husband keeps telling me that I can't fix all their problems. But I can't help but think if they would just listen, their lives would be so much easier. I just want to help them and not have them make the same mistakes I did. Is this so wrong?

—Sixty-five-year-old learned-the-hard-way mom

Most of the time, we offer advice based on only partial information. We don't really know what occurred yesterday, the day before, or moments ago that may be feeding into the situation at hand. We can't resist making a comment, though, not because we want to control the situation, or that we don't trust our children's judgment, but because we don't want them to make the same stupid mistakes we've made. Maybe it's time to learn that they will ask for advice when they need it, but more often they just want us to listen, not to judge, and to always be there for them.

If you think about recent conflicts you've had with your adult children, most of you would probably agree that they could have been avoided, and maybe you jumped over the net into their court when you shouldn't have. Here's what a seventy-eight-year-old mom thinks about it:

One day recently, I realized that I don't need to be my children's problem-solver any more. They are doing just fine. It was an awareness that has made both my life and their life and our relationship better. I used to hop in on any disagreement, give my advice, and get involved in the situation. I would lose sleep over their problems. I now realize that it's like giving advice to my girlfriend about her marriage. That pancake has two sides, and I only know one of them. The same thing is true with giving my children advice. I rarely have enough information to be objective, and it's just best I stay out of it. Now, I work really hard to only offer advice when asked, and then I do so with caution!

—Seventy-eight-year-old no-longer-offering-advice mom

☞ REALITY CHECK

The next time the tension is rising or there are problems with your adult children or in their lives and you're about to offer unsolicited advice, ask yourself these questions that many in our discussion groups thought helped them and their adult children improve their relationships:

1. How serious is the situation, really?

2. Will offering advice truly be helpful, or will it just make your adult child think you're a pain in the ass?

3. Do you fully understand the situation, or is there information you may not be privy to, perhaps something that you may not have seen or heard that may make the situation more complex than you realize?

4. Would someone else be a better advisor? Are you an expert on this issue, or do you just think you are?

5. Whose needs are you fulfilling by acting as an advisor: your child's or yours?

6. Most importantly, did your adult child ask for the advice? If not, maybe it's time to zip it up and get back on your own side of the net.

If you feel *absolutely* certain that you *absolutely* must offer advice, do it selectively and with kindness.

TIME TO PASS THE BATON

For many of our respondents, the realization that they are no longer the official head of their households is a difficult pill to swallow. They may still be the elders in their families, but they are no longer calling the shots. This can lead to conflicts. Parents may assume that their relationship with their adult children is more balanced than it is or that they are still in charge. It's almost as though the parents don't remember they're no longer raising their children.

Relationships between parents and children, like all relationships, change. Sometimes it happens quickly; at other times, it happens over an extended period of time. Regardless, it always happens. One day, we are no longer in charge of our children. Our respondents noted that sometimes they missed the signals. Comments regarding this power shift were sometimes serious, sometimes funny, but always insightful.

Here is what two of our respondents had to say:

Power shift—didn't even realize that I had power before, but I realize I don't have it now.

—Sixty-seven-year-old power-shifting grandma

I'm at the mercy of their whims. We see them when they want, not when we want.

—Seventy-four-year-old getting-a-grip grandpa

We discovered from our surveys and interviews that some parent–child relationships are based on power. The parents estab-lish rules when the children are growing up, with little input from them. In other families where power isn't such an issue, the children are able to call some of the shots. The relationship between the parent and adult child is more relaxed, because there's less need for the power to shift as the children get older. The parents and children are used to sharing ideas, thoughts, and decision-making.

Even in families where the power is more balanced, tensions, disagreements, and conflicts still occur. They do in any relationship that is valued, and the parent–adult child relationship is no exception. As expressed in the following comments, tension can create negative feelings on both sides.

I feel like I'm walking on eggshells when I'm around them for fear they will take the grandkids away from us if I don't do or say just the right thing.

—Seventy-one-year-old
doing-the-right-thing grandmother

They think I'm a bad influence on my grandkids…my house smells, my food choices aren't right, I don't follow their rules. Bummer!

—Sixty-seven-year-old smelly grandpa

Many respondents echoed the feelings of these grandparents. They felt that the younger generation had moved them to the sidelines and they were no longer the primary decision-makers in the family. The implication was, at times, that their children were ungrateful, thoughtless, and to blame for their lack of self-worth.

It wasn't a gentle passing of the baton...it seemed abrupt. We no longer made any decisions about our family's social activities...they were all predetermined for us. It made me wonder if I had lived my life like that...just making plans and assuming others would follow along, never asking others what they wanted to do. Now I wonder, were they traditions, or did we just lay down the law of what would happen next?

—Seventy-one-year-old traditional grandmother

My kids used to be really proud of me. My wife and I came from nothing and worked really hard to become well-educated and with good jobs and create a really nice family. Now, I don't feel comfortable around them. They don't really seem to like me anymore, but just tolerate me. I can tell they don't want me to be around their friends. I wonder when and why that has happened. Every kind gesture they make seems motivated more by responsibility than genuine desire.

—Seventy-seven-year-old uncomfortable grandfather

Experts explain that successful adaptation to old age requires successfully moving from one stage to the next. As developmental psychologist Erik Erikson tells us, in our final stage of development, we must take on a more supportive role.[26] We are no longer the ones making all the decisions. Those who continue to want to take the lead, to be center stage, may end up feeling unhappy, stagnant, and dissatisfied. More importantly, their relationships with their adult offspring may feel stressful and unfulfilling, as expressed by a few respondents in the above comments.

While some of our respondents blamed the younger generation for the change in their feelings of self-worth, other respondents told us that the changes in the family dynamics simply reflected the natural order of things and they were quite comfortable with the changes. Rather than having the leading role as elders, these parents of adult children were happy to fall into supporting roles as their children took the lead.

I am so proud of how my adult children have turned out. It's a real sense of relief and pride to know they are in charge of their own lives—to know they can come to me if they need advice, but to realize that they are the ones to determine when and if that should happen. I see some of my friends struggle with the change in their relationship with their adult children and it surprises me. I couldn't be

prouder, and even relieved that they are now in charge of
their own lives.

—Seventy-two-year-old real proud mom

Those who stepped off center stage and accepted more
supporting roles with their adult children were more likely to
have satisfying relationships with them and a greater sense of
self-worth overall. Many were glad to relinquish some power
and realized it was the natural order of life.

I have found that questioning my adult children's rationale
for doing things is an insult to their capabilities. So, I step
back and let it go. Should a conversation open in a peace-
ful moment when both parties are open to a conversation, I
ask them questions about how things are working out: "Is
there something I can do for you?" It may open up a mature
discussion. If not, I drop it. Patience pays off because it
preserves the relationship.

—Seventy-one-year-old patient mom

☞ REALITY CHECK

Figuring out what your relationship is or should be
with your adult children can be difficult. Maybe some

of these suggestions we uncovered from our respondents will be helpful:

1. Change is inevitable in every relationship. It's the natural order of things, so it's best to accept it.

2. Identify the most pressing issues for all family members and be sensitive to stressful periods in their lives.

3. You can continue to be a role model, an example of how to be a healthy, well-adjusted, and successful older person, and of the relationship others might want (or not want) with their own adult children. Remember, no matter how old your children are, they are still learning about relationships and life.

4. As you continue to age, you will be a role model of how to handle loss, conflict, and illness. If you don't have the strength to be your *best* because it's the best thing for you, do it because you are helping your children learn how to deal with these difficult situations.

5. Just as when they were young, they are *always* watching, and it matters more what you *do* than what you *say*.

DEALING WITH THE INEVITABLE

Now that we've established that tension and disagreements between us and our adult children are inevitable, the question is, how do we handle the discord? Anyone who has been successful in the workplace or in their home life has learned a thing or two about how to manage conflict. Some of us tend to forget the rules, though, when the conflicts are in our family.

Kira Birditt, an expert in interpersonal problems, has observed that when conflicts arise between aging parents and their adult children, the most successful people initially try to see the other person's perspective. As the tension level increases, however, some turn to destructive conflict-management strategies, such as yelling, name-calling, or unfair arguing tactics. It takes great strength of character not to lose our tempers. As most of us have learned, losing our temper is extremely ineffective. Even worse, according to Birditt, is refusing to talk at all.

Saying nothing at all surely avoids a conflict, but it sweeps problems under the rug, where they can grow and fester, or worse yet, bring about the end or cause a serious change in the relationship. Researchers tell us that while we may feel upset during an argument, avoiding a conflict can have negative effects that last a lifetime.

——— WHY WE AVOID CONFLICT ———

From our surveys and interviews, it became clear that some of us avoid conflicts for good reasons. Some had noted that their families of origin often resorted to yelling and name-calling during disagreements; thus, they were likely to avoid difficult conversations. Some have never had the experience of having a conflict resolved effectively. Not surprisingly, they avoided conflict whenever possible, often to the detriment of a relationship. Psychologists explain that if our families of origin dealt with conflict effectively, we are more inclined to engage in difficult conversations, while recognizing that disagreements may not always be easy to work through.

As Birditt suggests, the old adage "If you can't say something nice, don't say anything at all" isn't good advice for parents and adult children. Avoidance is not an effective strategy for dealing with significant family problems. If you've been employing negative conflict-management techniques, it's time to break that cycle. We hope the reality check below will offer some new conflict-management strategies for you to try.

☞ REALITY CHECK

One of the keys to dealing better with family conflict is being able to view the problem from the other person's perspective. These suggestions from several of our respondents might help the next time you and your adult child are in a potentially heated argument.

1. People often say and do things in an argument that they later regret. Don't take everything the other person says personally.

2. Your feelings may be hurt, but try to remove emotions from the situation and objectively look at the issue from the other person's viewpoint.

3. Attempt to find common ground. In any conflict, someone has to be the hero. Try to be that person. Don't be afraid to be the first one to say you're sorry; you'll probably never regret it.

4. There will be times when you will have to stand up for something you believe in. Only rarely should this be necessary, and the reason for doing so should be a valid one. Pick your battles carefully.

5. Finally, and unfortunately, there are some situations that are too unmanageable and/or mentally or physically abusive to accept. It's sometimes OK to end a relationship if that is the

best option to preserve your well-being. These situations are never easy, but sometimes allowing someone to leave your life truly is the best way to resolve conflict. If you need to go this route, you may want to seek professional help or support from friends and other family members for handling your hurt and disappointment.

No one should have to be a doormat in any relationship and certainly not in one with your adult children. However, it's sometimes better to be happy than right, right? In relationships with adult children, it may be better to forget about being right and instead focus on enjoying the relationship you have.

WHAT'S YOUR DEFINITION OF FAMILY?

Much research has been done on another source of conflict for older parents and their adult children: how each defines who is in their family. Many of the older parents we surveyed included their children and grandchildren in their definitions of their families but told us that their adult children's definitions of their own families would not include them. This was a source of tension for many respondents we surveyed. Members of several of our discussion groups told some poignant stories. A seventy-three-year-old grandfather, a sixty-nine-year-old grandmother, and a seventy-year-old grandfather summarized the negative feelings that some of our respondents had experienced.

My kids use language like "my family" and "our family," and they don't mean us. Just who do they think is my family if it is not them? I can't wait until they get to my age, when their own kids don't think of them as part of their family. It really hurts my feelings.

—Seventy-three-year-old had-his-feelings-
hurt grandfather

I once sent my Christmas cards out to all of my friends. Just like my friends' cards, the main focus was beauti-ful pictures of my grandkids. I remember my son saying something like "Why is your Christmas card full of pictures of my family?" Well, I guess that was because I thought they were my family too. That was a sad day for me.

—Sixty-nine-year-old had-a-sad-day grandmother

It's sad but true that, as we age, many of us want to be closer to our children, especially if we've generally been close to our children all of our lives. Yet this is when they may be most busy with their own families and careers. Our children may be *pulling away* just when many of us want to be closer, causing tension in the relationship.

I'm always playing catch with my grandson. It's the thing we do. He and I had been discussing for weeks about going to get him a new baseball glove. We just needed the right time to do it. We talked about exactly how it would look and where we would go to get it and how much better he could play... Then, one day, I went to see him and he told me his dad had gone with him to get the new ball glove. His dad said that was something that his family should do for him. I talked with my son about it and he said it was a "family" event. Guess I'm not part of the family. He was nice about it. He told me in a very kind, thoughtful way. I'm proud that we have the kind of relationship that he can tell me that, but I still wanted to go.

　　—Seventy-year-old baseball-playing grandfather

While we can imagine how these situations might have played out differently, perhaps more inclusively, adult children will establish boundaries that work best for them and their immediate families. And, as the baseball-playing grandfather noted above, they have every right to do so.

As in any successful relationship, boundaries between the parents and their adult children occasionally need resetting as circumstances change. And, as in other successful relationships, being flexible is often key.

☞ REALITY CHECK

As illustrated in the example above involving the baseball glove, relationships don't have to suffer when boundaries are clarified. Had there been no conversation between the son and his dad, the event could have signaled the beginning of a rift that seriously damaged the relationship. As it was, although the older dad felt excluded, he honored his son's right to choose how the event would unfold. Both parties have to be honest when boundaries are crossed so that any conflicts can be repaired. These accumulated suggestions from our respondents may help as you think about who your family is.

1. It's OK for your adult children to establish boundaries of acceptable behavior in their homes and with their children; in fact, it's healthy for them to do so.

2. It's also OK for you to challenge how your adult children define family, while recognizing that they hold all the cards on this one. Trust that you've given them strong values and respect them and their choices.

3. Stay on your side of the net. Just because you think your adult children might be making a mistake doesn't mean you should tell them so.

4. Remember, we continue to be role models to our children, whether they're preteens, teenagers, or adults, and that living our lives the best we know how and letting them watch is the best way to teach them.

ROLE REVERSALS: THERE'S NO REHEARSAL

American humorist Erma Bombeck was a household name for many of us. Much beloved as an author and columnist, her weekly syndicated newspaper column celebrated the joys and oddities of being a housewife, back in the days when most women were homemakers. She shared her life with her readers, and one of her stories speaks particularly to the changing relationship between some parents and their grown children.

Bombeck recalls she was driving her daughter to the

store one day when a car crossed directly in front of them. She slammed on the brakes and instinctively threw her arm across her daughter to protect her. Some years later, it was her daughter who was driving. She also had to hit the brakes hard to avoid an accident. This time, it was her arm that flew out to protect her mother, and Erma thought, *So soon.*

It does seem to come just that soon, and it's the natural order of things. Knowing that, however, doesn't make the transition any easier for us. Our three respondents quoted below show differing takes on the problem.

My son keeps asking when I'm going to move in with him and his family. I know I'm having difficulty managing everything, but I want to stay here. I've lived in this house for forty years. There's so much commotion in his home. They're all so busy, and everything's constantly in an uproar.

—Eighty-year-old independent mom

We came to a compromise, my daughter and I. After my wife died, I was rambling around the old house and finally had to admit I was lonesome. They had a spare room, but that wasn't going to work. It was about the size of a prison cell. Anyhow, I agreed to move into senior housing, where

I get my meals and there's transportation available when I need it. It took some time to adjust, but it was the right decision. I get to shoot the breeze with folks my own age and also have my privacy. My daughter was right. I raised a good one!

—Seventy-eight-year-old grateful dad

I lived in San Jose, California, for many years. It was a family joke that on Winchester Boulevard you could literally progress from independence to death in three easy steps. First there was the apartment complex, next to that was the convalescent hospital, and finally, next to that was the cemetery. It was funny but also a reminder about the way life goes.

—Sixty-five-year-old realistic guy

Living arrangements can definitely become issues of contention between parents and their grown children. For the adult children, it's often a decision of convenience to have their elderly parents living with or near them. For the elderly parents, however, living so close to their children can be perceived as another loss of their independence. Living together is always an option, of course, when both parties are amenable. Often, though, it's the grown children who are insisting and the parents who are resisting.

☞ REALITY CHECK

At some point, we're all going to need help with managing a home, keeping track of our finances, paying the bills, and getting around. Being proactive about making arrangements for assistance can head off these problems before they become overwhelming.

1. Have you given thought to what you'll do when taking care of your home becomes too much work for you? What options are available in your community?

2. If you're on good terms with your grown children, sit down with them and have a serious discussion about what you'd like to do when the time comes to move out of your home.

3. If you're determined to remain in your home, you can subscribe to a company that specializes in summoning help for you. You've likely seen the commercials for companies that provide a bracelet or necklace with a button you can push to connect you to an emergency hotline. You can continue to live alone, but help is immediately available if you need it. This option may help give your grown children peace of mind while preserving your independence.

Finances are sometimes a bone of contention between parents and their grown children. For some of our respondents, the time had come to stop being the First National Bank of Mom and Dad. For others, it was the grown children who were worried about their parents' financial health.

We've always been there for our kids, helping them out when they needed help. Sometimes it was just a few thousand, sometimes it was more. We bought our son a car when his bit the dust and he couldn't afford to buy a new one. Finally, we had to tell him no when he asked for our help for tuition to go back to school when he decided to change careers. His reaction wasn't pretty. It was also our fault. By giving him everything he wanted whenever he asked, he never had to take care of himself. Now he's nearly fifty, and it's like he's starting out for the first time. Our relationship is strained right now. He's not talking to us.

—Seventy-eight-year-old former bankers

Our kids call us every week to check in. They're not subtle about their intentions, either. My daughter is always asking if we have enough money. Always asking if we need anything. We're not rich, but we're comfortable. We've always paid off our credit cards every month. We own our home outright, and we're perfectly happy driving our ten-year-old car. We tried to raise our children with the same respect for a healthy financial life, and we succeeded. Sometimes, I think we over-succeeded!

—Sixty-six-year-old successful parents

☞ REALITY CHECK

Money issues are often at the heart of family discord. Arguments about finances can break marriages and strain relationships between adult children and their elderly parents. If you're having these problems with your adult children, it's never too late to work on solving the problems.

1. If you've always been generous with handouts, it's natural for your adult children to expect they'll continue indefinitely. Have a sit-down with them and explain the financial facts of life. If they don't accept the change in circumstances, give it time. Most will come around after they've had time to think about what you've said.

2. If your children are trying to push money on you or are getting too inquisitive about every

penny you have, it's also time to have a conversation. If they've expressed concern about your financial health, take it as proof that you have done a good job raising them.

3. Tell them you're proud of them and that if or when you need their help, you will let them know.

All relationships go through stressful times. When the stress involves our adult children, it seems like a whole new set of growing pains. Discussing the issues and coming to solutions that benefit everyone require time and patience, but the result is clearer expectations, increased understanding, and peace of mind for all.

MAKE IT THE BEST RELATIONSHIP POSSIBLE

It's easy to forget that our adult children may have very different perspectives than we do on a variety of life issues, including childrearing, marriage, and politics. They were brought up among peers different from ours, and they have had very different life experiences. Consequently, they may make decisions that differ from those we would make under similar circumstances.

Some of our respondents noted that they vehemently disagreed with their adult children's values and lifestyle choices. Those who were able to maintain a healthy relationship despite these different perspectives were able to establish boundaries within their own home and surroundings and learned to respect the boundaries that their children had established as well. For example, one respondent noted that her adult son loved to smoke pot and thought it was perfectly acceptable to do so in her home. The two ultimately agreed that he would not smoke when visiting her, but if she came to visit him and he chose to do so, that was his right and his boundary to set.

It's easy to forget that *all* parents have the capacity to instill shame, guilt, or fear in their children. We have more power than anyone else to serve up these emotions at any stage of our children's lives. We must guard against doing so. We've noted this earlier in this book, but it bears repeating: people may not remember what we say, but they will *always* remember how we made them feel. There is never a better time than now to start making our adult children feel accepted, loved, and respected.

You may be tempted to offer advice when it isn't solicited. Try not to move into problem-solving mode too quickly. It's a hard habit to break, but it's essential if you're going to have a healthy relationship with your adult children. Focus on *showing* them and *telling* them that you trust that they are fully capable of dealing with their own problems, that you are there to listen, to be supportive, and to love them. We bet you will find that doing so releases you from their problems and might make your life more peaceful.

Be proud of the new family traditions your adult children have created, even if they're different from your own or the way you think they should be. Remember how you worked so hard to make your children stand up for themselves when they were in school, how you encouraged them to challenge people in authority when something didn't seem fair? Now is the time to honor the lessons you taught them.

While the quotations from our respondents highlight the challenges common in parent–adult child relationships, many of the parents we interviewed told us about memorable times with their adult children and their families. Many viewed their adult children as their very best friends and noted that their proudest moments were related to how their children had grown into remarkable adults.

The best part of my life is watching my children and grand-children grow up and actually become successful adults.

—Seventy-seven-year-old watching grandpa

My daughter is my very best friend. One of the greatest joys of growing older is having her in my corner through every happy, sad, exciting new experience in my life.
—Sixty-nine-year-old daughter-is-her-best-friend gal

These are just two examples of the overwhelming number of positive comments our respondents made about their relationships with their adult children. And while aging parents are generally very aware of how important their relationships with their adult children are to their mental, physical, and psychological well-being, these relationships are important for the adult children as well. We all need to recognize the value in keeping these relationships meaningful and healthy.

Chapter 6

HEALTH, FITNESS, AND SELF-IMAGE

Do You Like What You See?

"You're in pretty good shape for the shape that you're in."

—Dr. Seuss

As a generation, we are healthier and living longer and generally better than past generations. The battles against heart disease and cancer continue, and we have confidence that future miracles in research await us. If these medical advances don't come in our lifetimes, we expect that our children and grandchildren will reap the benefits.

We've battled cigarettes and depression and strokes and pain and addictions. Some of us faced our struggles with fear, some with faith, some with grim determination, and some with a fatalistic resignation. We know that while we may be healthy today, there are no guarantees for tomorrow. The task then is to get real about our health and discover what optimal health looks like for us at this stage of life. Each one of our respondents had a unique story to tell and a different perspective on health.

—WHAT IS PERFECT HEALTH ANYWAY?—

Over the course of our lives, so much has happened and continues to happen in the field of medicine. We've gotten new hips and knees and even experienced organ transplants that in the 1950s would have been the stuff of science fiction films.

Two years ago, I got new knees. I was suffering the kind of pain requiring such an operation. I was mindful that my walking gait was awkward and my golf game was tanking, so I found the best surgeon (who took one look at my bone-on-bone knees X-ray and said, "Let's do this."). I am now a better golfer than I was three years ago, and I'm confident that I'll be a walker/golfer for many more years. My point: No need to go meekly into our seventies and eighties. Let's do what we can to be physically fit, even if an operation or two has to make it happen.

—Seventy-year-old better golfer now

If you want to keep moving, you need the equipment to make it possible. I was always active, but I noticed a few years back when I turned sixty that, frankly, it hurt to walk and was impossible to move any faster than a snail. That just wasn't acceptable. I opted for two total knee replacements and while rehab hurt like hell, now I can put on the miles without pain. Definitely made a difference in my life.

—Sixty-five-year-old with-better-equipment guy

I know this is a zero-sum game, but you can't focus on that. We're programmed to always think ahead—to plan for tomorrow. When you get sick, it messes up your plans. If you get really sick, it messes up your mind. I think the big risk is playing into the victim mentality. You know, those people who just can't accept that bad stuff happens. If I exercise and eat right, then I will live, I don't know, forever, I guess. These people make me crazy. You do the best you can with what you've got. It's just that simple. Getting older isn't a given, but if you're lucky enough to get this far, count your blessings and do whatever you can to keep on going.

—Seventy-eight-year-old zero-sum kinda guy

More than a decade ago, I had a brain tumor removed. It was a meningioma, the "best" kind of brain tumor to have. Can you imagine having a "good" tumor on your brain? It was benign. My head has a dip on the side where they did the surgery, but I am alive! Then, ten years later, I had a heart attack. Now, I thought, what's going on here? I've done my time, I had major surgery on my brain thirteen years ago. It's someone else's turn! But no, it was my turn again. And once again, I was very fortunate...no major blockage found, and no stents or surgery required. But after this heart attack, I was afraid...afraid to do some of the things I had always done, afraid I would have another one and it would kill me. And I was sad...sad because if I died, would anyone miss me? Would anyone even know I was gone? And then I realized I had to start living again because life is short; we are all going to die sometime. I am not ready, but it is out of my control... so I am enjoying each day to the best of my ability! Yes, I have bad days, even some really bad days, but I have more good days, and even great days! Life is short... I'm going to make the best of it!

—Sixty-eight-year-old
making-the-best-of-it gal

Dr. Christopher Meckel, nationally recognized orthopedic surgeon in Monterey, California, shared his views on health and aging during our interview when he told the story of a professor he had while studying medical anthropology at the University of California, Berkeley. This Berkeley professor was a visiting professor from London and apparently bore a strong resemblance to Dr. Andrew Weil, albeit with a British accent. Early in the course, the professor said he was going to introduce the concept that perfect health is an irrational concept and that living in a pain-free condition with a perfect interaction with our environment is not achievable. He called it *illth* to represent the state of ill health, or imperfect health, as being normal. Dr. Meckel remembers having a difficult time initially accepting this notion, but as he continued to consider it over the many years of his medical training, he eventually accepted the weighty truth of the concept.

According to Dr. Meckel, "We are rarely in a state of perfect health, which is normal. Perfect health really is a myth, and if we could look at health with a bit more objectivity, we would probably be less emotional when something *does* go wrong. Our expectations would be more reasonable, and we wouldn't be so taken aback when we have a pain or require surgery of some sort. If we *get real* about health, we would think, instead, 'I'm glad there is a solution for that pain that I am experiencing.'"

DEVELOPING REASONABLE
EXPECTATIONS ABOUT HEALTH

There's an old saying that "Health is wealth." It's true. Good health is priceless, and if we want to remain active in this last quarter of our lives, it's important to make the decision to take better care of ourselves. As Dr. Meckel noted, there is no such thing as being in perfect health. There's always some problem that arises, either big or small, that we need to address throughout our lives, but regardless of what the problems are, we have some degree of control, and it's never too late to make positive changes. In the following anecdotes, we can see who is being proactive and who is playing the waiting game.

> *I worry about my health (not enough to do much about it, I must admit). I don't want to end up in a nursing home or an assisted living place. I'd like to stay in my own home, but I don't want to be a burden.*
>
> —Seventy-four-year-old staying-in-his-home guy

Worrying is a waste of time and energy, and it doesn't help any situation. The realization that something isn't right or that we're not doing what we should be doing may be the first step in the decision-making process, but if we get stuck there, we're never going to deal with the problem that's causing the worry. The respondent above is engaging in some wishful thinking and hasn't yet decided to take action. Until he does, nothing will change, and he'll remain stuck in the worry zone.

I never thought I'd have trouble walking, and everything involves walking, so right now it's hard to get enthusiasm going when I know I can't walk for even garage sales, let alone a fair or anything like that. My son took me to a professional baseball game. I loved it but took two days to recover and I know I really slowed him down. I just have to come to terms with moving more slowly, but it's hard. I try to remember my husband and the many talks we had. One I remember was when he talked about his body not working; he hadn't been able to walk for a few months. He said that was the hardest ever for him. His mind came up with a list of things he wanted to do that day and then he'd open his eyes and remember he couldn't walk or do anything he had planned. His mind was still alive, but his body was already in his grave. I understood then as he had been so active, but I doubly understand now since I'm almost in the same boat. There is nothing one can do about this and I know I need to settle it in my mind. Some days I'm settled better than others! In the meantime, I try to enjoy each day as much as

I can, try to find something funny every day and pray each
night that I wake up in heaven.

—Seventy-seven-year-old in-the-same-boat-now wife

There's a great deal to think about in this respondent's
story. Her main physical problem involves difficulty walking.
She's tried to keep up with the pace of her younger years,
but she has discovered she can't. It takes too much out of her.
However, her reflection on this—"There is nothing one can
do about this"—reveals a deeper problem. She feels that she is
a burden to her son: "I know I really slowed him down." Her
solution is to give up on walking, look for the bright spots in
her day, and wait to die.

So, what is the answer here? Her son has tried to get her
out of the house. His choice of activity, however, didn't help
much. The lengthy walk to the stands, the endless stairs to
climb before reaching a hard seat, and reversing the process
after the game was over only reinforced her conclusion that she
was done with the outside world.

Her son shouldn't give up or give in. He should, however,
slow his pace. He doesn't need to move so quickly when
he's with his mother. Also, has he taken her to the doctor to
determine what's causing her difficulty in walking? If the
problem is arthritis, is she a candidate for knee replacement or

hip replacement surgery? Will physical therapy help restore some of her strength and agility? Until he and his mother have the answers, they won't be able to address them. If, indeed, walking is no longer an option, power chairs can provide an open door back into the world. Many people have used these assistive devices since childhood and live full, active lives.

She shouldn't give up on life because she's having trouble walking, and she should never think that she's a burden for slowing her son down. She carried him for nine months; it's his turn to carry her.

The anecdotes from the respondents below show positive, proactive approaches to dealing with the realities of health concerns. We're not young anymore, and we can't do what we did when we were young. We can, however, discover activities that increase our stamina and that our bodies can tolerate. Perfect health, as noted above, is a myth at any age. Fitness and good health, however, are often within our reach.

Our health has been good so far. I go to the gym (my new job) three times a week, sometimes more. My husband feels taking care of the yard and the house is enough exercise, so I gave up on him joining me in the gym. Our weight could be better and our stamina is OK, but my knees are shot from doing high-impact dance aerobics years ago, and it's very annoying I can't do that now. I do the cross-trainer, bike, and elliptical, but I feel doing aerobics and Zumba are a better workout. I want to try one of the Zumba classes again soon, even if I can only do part of it.

—Sixty-six-year-old Zumba gal

I always took good health for granted; maybe I was even cocky about it, but then I got hammered with a cancer diagnosis. Really hit me hard, but I came through it and now I have a healthy respect for health. I do what I can to make sure I stay healthy. It changes you, cancer. Maybe any serious diagnosis does. You never look at life the same way again, and you never take good health for granted again, either. So, getting older doesn't mean as much to me as living every day I'm given. Doesn't matter if I'm sixty or eighty. Each day counts, and the calendar means nothing.

—Seventy-one-year-old each-day-counts guy

I finally bought a real pair of sneakers. I never wore real sneakers, felt they were too clumsy, but I like them for the gym. I'm amazed at the agility of those in my fitness class who are in their seventies and older. When I was younger, I still couldn't do some of the things they're able to do. Being active is important. It seems people my age and older are doing more these days than ever before.

—Sixty-six-year-old sneakers kinda gal

We spend our winters at a senior resort community in Arizona. It's not possible to do nothing there. There's something to do every day, and we've found that the more we do, the easier it is to do more. I took up golf, and my partner swims every morning. It's easy to fit in when you're doing what everyone else is. I never knew older people could be so active. It makes me feel younger!

—Seventy-six-year-old can't-do-nothing gal

What do these four respondents have in common? The youngest is sixty-six, the oldest is seventy-six. That's a ten-year span, and at this stage of the game, ten years is a healthy chunk of time. It's not their age; it's their attitude. Our Zumba gal is open to trying new activities; our cancer survivor has a new, positive outlook on life; our exercise gal bought herself a new pair of shoes so she can dive into new activities; and our snowbird has taken up a new sport and discovered an important truth about health: the more you do, the more you can do.

☞ REALITY CHECK

"Never, never, never give up."
—Winston Churchill

How much control do you have over your physical abilities? Take a few minutes to take stock. We can't do all the activities we did at the same pace we did when we were young, but what *can* you do today to keep active?

1. Make the decision to do some form of physical activity every day.

2. Do you walk? Do you bicycle? What are your favorite physical activities? Gardening is the number one hobby in America. If you have difficulty bending, there are stools you can use to get a front-row seat for your roses or your vegetables while you tend to them. (You will find resources in the appendix.)

3. Do you enjoy walking? You don't have to set a record pace. Just getting out in the fresh air and meandering around your neighborhood on your own schedule will do wonders for you. There's no time clock to punch. If it takes you an hour to walk around the block, so what? Enjoy the walk. You will see what others don't.

> 4. Many senior centers offer fitness classes. Activities include stretching, swimming, and a variety of low-impact aerobics activities.

DO REGULAR MAINTENANCE

Through the comments above, some of our respondents shared more than their outlook on physical exercise. They also shared their outlook on life. If you have trouble moving, you move less, you do less, you see less, and your world gets smaller. It can be easy to judge others when our own health is still good, but the true test is how we react when it starts to decline.

I believe in the old saying, "Walk a mile in someone else's shoes before you pass judgment." It's true. Then if you find out you still can't relate to them or they just won't do anything to improve their lives, you're a mile away and you're wearing their shoes.

—Sixty-seven-year-old shoe thief

Sometimes, when our health has taken a downturn, it's easier to throw in the towel, to chalk it up to the inevitable aspects of getting older. It takes determination and grit to accept the limitations, whether for the short or long term, and make the conscious decision to not give up on life.

"You're only as young as you feel." I hear this all the time, and whoever thought up this clinker must have just taken a few too many pain pills. Why? Because if you follow this way of thinking, you'd feel about seventy in the morning, forty about midday, and about ninety before cocktail hour. And don't forget to figure in all the stressors life throws at you during the day. I'm not trying to sound negative, just realistic. Here's my explanation.

I've been pretty fortunate. Sure, I've had some medical issues, but for the time being, there's nothing serious going on. Still, I no longer jump out of bed in the morning ready to face the day. I open my eyes. If that part goes well, then I take an inventory of my remaining body parts. I do a little stretching. If I don't get a charley horse in my calf, I'm good for getting out of bed.

Coffee next. Now everything is going well. All my parts are in sync. If the rest of nature's processes work according to plan, I'll be in even better shape after that. Not sure I feel young, but I'm feeling OK. It takes longer to loosen up than it used to, in fact everything I do takes longer than it used to. But that's OK too. I've got more time to get things done. When I think about the pace of my younger years, I marvel at the man I used to be. He was a real dynamo. But he is now me, and he's learned to slow down and appreciate what the day has to offer. And I don't dwell on the "age as numbers" game. I'm just taking life one day at a time.

—Seventy-three-year-old OK-to-slow-down guy

As we age, there often comes an awareness that we're walking the same path as our parents before us. With our increased understanding of the role that genetics plays in our physical health, it's only natural to make comparisons. It's important to realize, however, that there have been many medical breakthroughs in the past few decades, so what ailed your parents or grandparents may be fixable or even preventable today.

Last May, I celebrated my seventy-second birthday. It was great, but I couldn't help but see my dad's face all day long. He died of a heart attack a week after his seventy-second birthday, and I got to tell you, it sort of took some of the happy out of that birthday. I kept wondering if the death fairy was planning on making me a visit next week. It took me a little while to get over it. I didn't die. And that's when

I finally realized that there is no magic number that will have your name on it. I have advantages he didn't. I keep a close check on my blood pressure and my weight. He didn't, and that might have made the difference.

—Seventy-two-year-old escaping-the-death-fairy guy

This respondent is keeping on top of issues that are important to his health. It all boils down to maintenance and upkeep. Just as you change the oil and rotate the tires on your vehicle, you also have to do the routine maintenance on your own body. If you have a family history of coronary artery disease, it's important to monitor your blood pressure and keep up to date on your prescription medications and exercise program. Our respondent understands his risk and is determined to keep on top of his health, unlike the husband of the respondent below.

I love this inscription on a tombstone: "I told you I was sick." It proves the point I'm always trying to make to my husband. He tells me I'm a hypochondriac because I go to the doctor when something bothers me. I tell him I'd rather not live with any more pain or discomfort than I have to, and I trust my body to tell me when something isn't right. He just shakes his head.

Can I get him to go to the doctor? No. He's had a cough for the past three months and just ignores me. What can I do? He tells me I'm nagging him. He flat-out won't go. He thinks it's some sort of show of strength to tough it out, but it's not getting any better. And he smokes. I think he's afraid to find out what might be wrong.

—Seventy-three-year-old nagging wife

COPING WITH CAREGIVING

When we can no longer care for ourselves, others must assume that responsibility. If that person is a member of our family, the emotional toll can be great.

My wife has dementia. It's gotten pretty bad, and if I didn't have the internet, I think I'd go nuts. There's a support group for caregivers that I belong to. I proba-bly shouldn't say this, but I've started correspond-ing with a lady whose husband is in the final stages of Alzheimer's. I'd never abandon my wife, but it gets pretty hard sometimes, being all alone. She's not really herself anymore. It's like she died and her body forgot to go with her. I miss her.

—Seventy-six-year-old grieving husband

Being the caregiver for a spouse or partner is hard work. It's hard on the person with the disability, and it's doubly hard on the caregiver. And when the disabled person is elderly, the situation isn't likely to get any better, which can make the caregiver feel hopeless.

My husband had a stroke last year. He can't talk, and it frustrates him. I have to do the translating for him and he hates being dependent on me. He doesn't want to go anywhere anymore. He doesn't want people to see him like this. I'm afraid to leave him alone, but I would love to have just a little free time to myself. That would make it so much easier.

—Eighty-four-year-old desperate wife

Our first experiences with caregiving usually involve our children. We practice on them! But children mature, grow up, and (usually) move away. As they get older, they require less and less hands-on attention. Our role naturally changes from caregiver to advisor and supporter as they move toward independence. With a disabled or ill spouse or partner, we take on the role of caregiver again as we get older.

The situation can be even more difficult when we're caring for an older person because the prognosis is not likely a good one. There's no end in sight, or there is an end, but not one we want to think about. Wishing that our suffering loved one would pass away, while perfectly normal, often leads to guilt. Guilt can arise because we silently wish that the person we're caring for will die, freeing us from the burden of care. Guilt can also arise from selfishly wondering if the end will come soon enough for us to have a chance to live without being tied down providing hours of care. It's an odd sensation to make the connection between the end we don't want to think about and our complex feelings about it.

It's only human to have these feelings. Of course, we mostly just wish the ill or disabled person would recover. That's what we'd really like.

Caregiving takes a toll on us physically and emotionally. It's strenuous, stressful work, and may lead to caregiver stress syndrome. Caregiver stress syndrome, or what is more casually called *caregiver stress*, occurs when a caregiver is the constant and often sole caregiver of a chronically ill spouse or partner. Sleep issues, weight gain or loss, depression, a compromised immune system, and heart disease risks are some of the symptoms.[27]

A study by the American Psychological Association showed that caregivers are more likely to suffer from a chronic illness than the general population (82 percent versus 61 percent).[28] As further evidence of the toll that caregiving can take, 34 percent of the caregivers in this study evaluated their own health as fair or poor, versus 20 percent for the general population. The bottom line is that stress builds, and the caregiver's health is affected. A caregiver who becomes ill can't provide care. It's that simple. Older adults who find themselves in the role of caregiving should carefully monitor their own physical and mental well-being, and seek help or support if necessary.

☞ REALITY CHECK

Anyone who has ever flown on an airplane has heard the safety talk given by the flight attendants before takeoff. The part about the oxygen mask dropping out of the ceiling compartment has relevance for us here. You're told that if you're traveling with children or anyone who needs your care, put your own mask on first and then to tend to the needs of your charges. The reason is obvious: if you aren't able care for yourself, you won't be able to take care of anyone else.

What can you do if you find yourself struggling in a caregiver role?

1. There is support available for caregivers, from in-home services to day care centers. You'll be

able to get some restorative time, your health will improve, and you'll return to your duties with a clearer focus and a healthier body.

2. Contact your local senior center, your doctor's office, the Alzheimer's Association, or any of the other agencies listed in the appendix at the end of this book.

3. As caregiver, you may often get the sense that it is all give and no take. Remember to take care of yourself while you are taking care of others. Put your own oxygen mask on first.

WHAT IF THERE'S NOTHING TO BE DONE?

Sometimes, the time to pay the piper comes more quickly than we imagined or were prepared for. If we know we are at risk for certain diseases, if we engaged in risky behaviors in our youth, if we have succumbed to the pervasive advertisements touting one brand of cigarette over another, if we have done anything that might have predisposed us to one or more medical conditions, we may arrive at the point when the tests ordered by the doctor give us news we don't want to hear. Then what?

Sometimes, there is a course of treatment that will give us more time. Isn't that really all we're looking for at this stage of our lives, anyway? Should you luck out, should there be a course of treatment that gives you more time, then you have one more task to complete. What will you do with the time you've been given? Not everyone is so fortunate. For some, the end comes quickly, and there is no time to tie up loose ends.

Cancer. I had no idea I'd get cancer. Never even gave it a thought. But I smoked all my life. Cigarettes came in the GI ration kits—even endured the jokes about lighting one cigarette from the last one—but it's no joke. So, basically, I f——ed up. What the hell was I thinking? I wasn't thinking anything. Now I've got to get everything done soon. I'm leaving my wife and my grandkids. I sure will miss seeing them grow up. But there's nobody to blame but myself. I let them all down.

—Seventy-five-year-old regretful guy

I knew my mother and her sisters had heart issues, but I didn't think I would have their problems. I went to the cardiologist every six months, monitored my blood pressure, and tried to watch my diet. Now, I'm in heart failure. I'm not a candidate for a transplant because I have some liver disease. I'm trying to deal with all this and make peace, but I'm a little, no, a lot scared.

—Seventy-four-year-old frightened grandmother

This time will come for all of us. How we will cope depends to a large degree on our support system—our beliefs or our faith, our family and friends, and the strength of our own character. Accepting this reality is one of the toughest tasks we face. Death is part of life. However, we've become isolated to some extent from death in today's society, and we have developed a host of euphemisms for the word. For past generations, though, death was a frequent visitor. It took women in childbirth, children, young adults, and the elderly without discrimination. Today medical advances have vastly reduced mortality in the young and postponed it in the elderly. It can be easy to pretend it doesn't exist or that it's "out there" somewhere, far away. The reality is, however, that our lives will someday end. We cannot escape it, but we can decide to face it as best we can. That final confrontation can be easier if we have lived our lives the best we were capable of doing. And for that reason, we need to live while we're alive.

WELCOME TO MEDICARE

Signing up for Medicare has become one of our rites of passage, sort of like graduating from high school, a bar mitzvah or confirmation, or a wedding. You know you've arrived at old age when the brochures for Medicare enrollment begin piling up in your mailbox. And you need an advanced degree in government-speak to wade through them all. Whatever provider you decide to accept, you need to decide it on time, or you will carry the demerit of a late penalty for the rest of your life. So, what can you expect from Medicare, and how can you navigate the system?

The annual physical is like walking through the portal of one of the gates of hell. Always has been in my opinion, but after you hit sixty-five and Medicare kicks in, you no longer have an annual physical. Nope. You have an annual wellness exam. Your first one is your introduction to the system, and good luck from there on out. You even get an "end-of-life counseling session" to add to your misery. The doc's assistant asked me what my plans were, and I told her I'd probably die. She wrote that on the form. I think it's on my permanent record somewhere in the vaults of the Pentagon now. Along with the Ark of the Covenant from Indiana Jones.

—Sixty-seven-year-old
been-through-the-gates-of-hell guy

A sense of humor is a powerful weapon, as our respondent above has discovered, and it can make dealing with the requirements of Medicare's procedures easier. The wellness exam differs from the annual physical in several regards. There's the end-of-life plans, as noted above. There's also an instruction sheet for you to tack to the fridge that tells first responders whether to resuscitate you if you have a heart attack. And, to determine whether you're going senile, you're asked to draw a clock and indicate a specific time using the big hand and the small hand. You are also told three words that you will be asked to recall at the end of your appointment. If you weren't feeling old when you showed up for your appointment, you'll definitely feel old when it's over.

The burden is on the patient. Wading through forms, making decisions about choosing supplemental plans, and dealing with changes in rules and regulations are all require-ments of Medicare, and it falls to the enrollee to tackle all of them.

What happens with people who can't understand all the forms and paperwork? It got me to thinking about what's going to happen with me when I can't keep it all straight any longer. I've still got most of my marbles, but I see a time when my thinking is going to slow down and it's going to get more and more difficult to make sense of it all. What am I going to do then?

—Seventy-five-year-old still-got-his-marbles guy

Once I got through the enrollment process, I've had good experiences with Medicare. But I think I'm one of the lucky ones. I got to stay with my old doctor. Her practice doesn't kick you out when you hit sixty-five. My buddy wasn't so fortunate. He moved from Louisiana and had a really tough time finding a new doctor here in Washington. So many don't take folks on Medicare. It's a stressful situation.

—Sixty-six-year-old happy-to-stay-with-his-doctor guy

The physician–patient relationship is an important one. It can seem almost a violation of trust to reach the age of sixty-five and discover that your doctor will no longer provide care for you and you must find one who will. It's just one more reminder of how life changes and how we must continue to adapt as we age.

Medicare provides valuable services to patients: finding participating physicians; educating on the various supplemental options; and addressing general concerns and questions about the program. But to obtain this information, you need internet access and the ability to navigate their website.

Sometimes I feel my way of life is slipping away. All that was familiar is gone. Sometimes I feel isolated—like I'm not a part of anything any longer. Medicine has definitely improved. I wouldn't be here if it hadn't, but it's become less personal. I never know which doctor I'm going to see, and she spends all her time on her tablet, writing. She hardly makes eye contact. When we were young, the doctor came to the house. Dr. Howard's practice was just across the street, but house calls was what they did (back then).

It's sure different now. I feel as if I'm wasting their valuable time. I get my fifteen minutes and then they're on to the next patient. She wouldn't even recognize me if she saw me on the street. Dr. Howard couldn't do what doctors can do today, but he cared about us and isn't that a kind of medicine?

—Eighty-two-year-old not-liking-the-new-system gal

Medicine is practiced differently today than in times gone by. The personal aspects have undergone considerable change, and while many doctors strive to maintain a close relationship with their patients, many others are overwhelmed by the sheer numbers of patients, the amount of paperwork required of them, and increasingly, pressures to increase the profit margin of their corporate-owned practices.

BALANCE MATTERS

Fear of falling becomes a real concern as we age, because taking a tumble can result in life-altering consequences. A broken hip is a serious injury, and among the oldest in our group may prove fatal. The National Institutes of Health report that many deaths from falls are due to complications after a hip fracture. In fact, one in five people who incur a fractured hip will die within a year of the injury. This statistic holds true for women as young as sixty-five.[29] As a result, even the most athletic of us find ourselves exercising a bit more care when we are on uneven ground or rocky terrain.

I used to be so sure-footed. I'd cross the brook behind our house stepping from rock to rock without a care. Never worried about falling. But now I don't even try to do it. At some point fear of falling entered the picture and it stole my joy. I don't want to risk injury. What if I broke my hip? I never would have imagined that would become my anti-risk mantra, but it has, and it bothers me. I've become cautious. I miss my younger self that would throw caution to the winds and take chances, because now I can't afford to do that. What if?

—Seventy-seven-year-old more-cautious gal

Last week I tripped over something while outside a fast-food restaurant and really got banged up. I had to have stitches, bruised my ribs, hurt my hand, so I see a future where I'll pay more attention to where I'm stepping and

gladly take assistance from others. This is my wake-up call.
My introduction to a new stage in life, and I'm not sure that
I like it all that much.

—Seventy-four-year-old paying-attention-now gal

We've all heard the advertisement catchphrase—and it's become more of a joke in our society—but "I've fallen and I can't get up" is no laughing matter. It's a fact of getting older. We need to be more aware of our surroundings and pay close attention to where we plant our feet when we're walking.

☞ REALITY CHECK

Get rid of the scatter rugs and make your environment friendly to your aging body. Think safety first.

1. What steps can you take to make your home safer for you?

2. Do you have handrails in your bathroom so you can get in and out of the tub easily?

3. If your home has more than one level, do you have handrails to help you climb and descend the stairs? Do you know how many stairs there

are to the next level? Memorize this number in case there is a power outage.

Making concessions as we age isn't negative thinking. It's practical thinking. And the saying "It's not the years but the mileage" is only partially true. Think of it the way one of our respondents did.

If you've got a low-mileage 1920 Ford coupe, you've got an old car with low miles. You can call it vintage, antique, classic— whatever, it's still an old car. Granted, if you've taken good care of it and haven't scrimped on the maintenance, it's going to purr like a kitten. A very old kitten. And finding parts isn't easy, if you don't want to go the aftermarket route.

If you've taken care of your body over the years, and if you've been blessed with good genes (like that Ford coupe), then you've done well. But you're still old. And that's not such a bad thing. Maybe you ought to start thinking of yourself as vintage or classic. And you're luckier, because the replacement parts they have today are state-of-the-art. Nothing wrong with that. Henry Ford used state-of-the-art parts when he began production. Something to remember.

—Seventy-four-year-old vintage sorta guy

THE VITALITY TWINS: DIET AND EXERCISE

As we age and our metabolism slows down, we require fewer calories to get through the day. If we continue to eat at sixty the same way we did at thirty, we're going to pack on the pounds. It doesn't seem fair, but fairness has nothing to do with it. If we're going to feel better and move more easily, we need to make changes to ensure we stay within the bounds of a reasonable weight. There are other benefits to a healthy diet and exercise besides a slimmer body—increased stamina and a strengthened immune system come along with it.

How can I still be worrying about my weight at age seventy-two? It seems a bit silly. I know I have lost three hundred pounds throughout my life...ten pounds at a time, up and down. Is there no learning going on at all in my life? Now that I'm seventy-two, should I finally stop worrying about my weight? Can I ever stop battling the bulge? Yet, now more than ever, I feel even better when I am thin. My bones, my muscles, my face...everything still feels so much better when I'm thinner. It's not about my looks anymore, it's about how I feel.

—Seventy-two-year-old battling-the-bulge gal

Health is wealth at any age, but you've got to be willing to make some changes and compromises. Obesity is uncomfortable, and it's also the invitation for a host of physical ailments: heart disease, diabetes, joint pain, certain types of cancer, and high blood pressure and high cholesterol, which bring increased chances of heart attack and stroke. It makes you wonder why it's so hard to say no to that bacon guacamole Swiss burger with fries and a large soft drink.

It's also important to pair that healthy diet with some physical activity.

WHAT ABOUT EXERCISING?

More to the point, what exactly *is* exercising and how does it differ from being physically active? Do old people really need to exercise? The answer is yes. Exercise has, at its core, a purpose: to improve physical fitness. Physical activity is simply any movement of the body that may or may not improve physical fitness. Using your thumbs to text someone is a physical activity. It's not likely, however, to improve your overall health and well-being. If, however, you put on your sneakers, head out the door, and walk around the block, you're exercising. You've got a purpose: to increase your stamina and support your immune system. You also may meet friends or neighbors along the way and exchange pleasantries. That is also good for your health. People who maintain their social connections are generally healthier than those who remain isolated.

I was always physically active, and still am, but it takes longer to get going. Exercising and moving the body parts are critical. I have always associated with people older than myself, so I think I had a good idea of what was coming. People that I associate with who are my age or older do not view themselves as old. Self-image is crucial to the state of your health and well-being. It all comes down to attitude.

—Eighty-four-year-old with attitude

The less you do, the less you can do. You can't let up. It's true: Use it or lose it. My weekends never involved sports or physical activities. Instead, I opted for taking it easy. Exercise wasn't fun, but something I knew I needed to do to be able to keep my joints moving. I became the King of Procrastination.

Now, I work hard at staying healthy. I exercise every day and completed my first 10K at seventy-one. I like to cook and eat healthy (most of the time). I firmly believe you have to take care of your body if you want it to take care of you.

—Seventy-five-year-old taking-care-of-his-body guy

☞ REALITY CHECK

Yes, exercise is hard work, but there is satisfaction in a job well done, and once you get into the habit, it's not so hard to keep going. How can you stay motivated? Here are some suggestions:

1. Get a dog, and get some exercise while you exercise Fido. It's also a great way to meet people and have interesting conversations. People with dogs are often considered more approachable.

2. Call a friend and make a standing date for a daily walk. The interaction will clean the cobwebs out of your brain, give your metabolism a gentle push, and help keep you healthy.

3. Contact your local senior center, ask what activities they sponsor, and sign up.

THE MIND–BODY CONNECTION

Health is a complex issue, involving both the body and the mind. Usually, though, we tend to concentrate mostly on the state of our physical health and ignore the body's relationship with the mind. There's still a stigma attached to mental health issues, and the jokes abound. Some of them are funny, often because there is a grain of truth embedded within.

> *With my current state of mind, I decided to change my computer login password to "incorrect." Then when I type in the wrong password, my computer will say your password is "incorrect."*
>
> —Seventy-six-year-old savvy geek guy

This respondent is having difficulty with recall. He's found a clever way to get around the problem, but nevertheless, he's aware that his memory is not as sharp as it used to be.

Just as people used to shy away from talking about polio, cancer, or AIDS—as if the mere mention of the words might be contagious—a stigma persists today around problems associated with the mind, such as Alzheimer's disease and Parkinson's. The human brain is an incredibly complex structure and we are only at the beginning stages of fully understanding how it works. Simply put, the human tendency is to fear what we don't understand. Because we are afraid we'll develop dementia or another debilitating mental condition, we avoid talking about it, hoping somehow the threat will just go away. It's a useless coping strategy. Talking about our fears is necessary if we're going to conquer these diseases.

There's a wide spectrum of what's considered normal when scientists talk about cognitive impairment as we age. Forgetfulness, for example, is a daily companion. So now we keep lists. We used to be able to keep everything we needed to remember in our minds, but those days are gone. Now, we add a new problem to the forgetfulness—figuring out where we put the list.

We joke about it, but it's sort of a whistling-past-the-graveyard kind of humor. "Out of all the things I have lost, I miss my mind the most," Mark Twain is supposed to have said. Where did I put my…glasses, keys, coffee? But what if it's not just forgetfulness, but the onset of something more insidious? What if it's Alzheimer's? How can you tell the difference, and more importantly, what can you *do* if you are anxious about it? If you're worried, that worry is going to affect your health.

It can be helpful to keep a diary. Keep track of your forgetfulness. Is there a pattern or is it random? Are you forgetting names? Forgetting what you were doing? Whatever you experience, write it down. Of course, keeping track of the diary is a whole different issue, but maybe all you need is a piece of paper stuck to the fridge with a magnet. Now, if you can't keep track of where your refrigerator is, you've got a problem.

If you're worried about a spouse or partner's mental state, be less visible about your recordings. A small notebook should suffice. Then, if what you've written troubles you, make an appointment to discuss your concerns with your doctor. And don't forget to take the diary to the appointment.

About memory—I don't remember everything like I used to. That's why I make lists, also use a calendar at my desk to mark appointments and events down. My mind has a way of sifting through what people say and trying to hold onto what seems the most important. The rest I can forget about completely or ask about later. Yes, at times it's hard to find items around the house, also to remember names, but it seems to me I never was very good at either before. I can't expect miracles.

—Seventy-five-year-old list-making guy

Keeping yourself mentally active is just as important as keeping your body active. If you're a crossword or jigsaw puzzle fan, if you enjoy number games, if you enjoy learning of any kind, you'll be giving your mind the workout it needs to keep at its best. The mind–body connection is powerful, for sure, but there's also another aspect to this equation. Changes in life circumstances can also impact our emotional health, bringing feelings of loneliness or a sense that life has become pointless.

── IS IT LONELINESS OR DEPRESSION? ──

"Have You Ever Been Lonely?" is the title of an old country song sung by Patsy Cline and Jim Reeves.[30] The answer, of course, is certainly. We've all been lonely at one time or another, but loneliness, while common in the elderly, is not the same as depression.[31] And being alone is not the same as being lonely. In fact, many older people live alone, either by choice or because of the death of a spouse or partner.

I've been alone over sixty years now. My husband died young, and I never remarried. I never had children. I'm comfortable in my home. I have friends, go to various activities, and I travel once in a while. Of course, there are times when I'm lonely, but this passes. I know some women who are still married and they're more alone in their marriages than I have ever been living by myself. When I do get a little down, I get out of the house and go do something. I'm lucky enough to still be active.

—Ninety-year-old not-lonely gal

Alone. Loneliness. Depression. What's the difference among these three terms? Being alone simply means that you're by yourself. The qualifier here, though, is that you're by yourself by *choice*. You don't have to be alone if you don't want to be alone.

Being lonely means you feel you don't have any options. You're by yourself but don't want to be. You wish you had someone with you. You feel friendless, abandoned, and unloved.

Depression is more serious than loneliness; it is a medical condition that can be treated. So if your loneliness becomes overwhelming, you are at risk for developing depression.

Here is the National Institute of Mental Health's list of symptoms of depression:

1. Persistent sad, anxious, or "empty" mood
2. Feelings of hopelessness or pessimism
3. Feelings of guilt, worthlessness, or helplessness
4. Loss of interest or pleasure in hobbies and activities
5. Decreased energy, fatigue, feelings of being "slowed down"
6. Difficulty concentrating, remembering, making decisions
7. Difficulty sleeping, early-morning awakening, or oversleeping
8. Appetite or weight changes
9. Thoughts of death or suicide, suicide attempts
10. Restlessness, irritability
11. Persistent physical symptoms

So, what causes depression? There can be many causes. The longer you live, the likelier you are to experience the death of friends and family. The depression this can cause is not survivor's guilt but stems from the sense that your world is shrinking. And, in many cases, there's great sadness from losing someone you love.

Also, the older you get, the likelier you are to become ill—another factor that can lead to depression. In fact, depression is a symptom of several conditions, including Parkinson's, hypothyroidism, and heart disease.[32]

Some prescription medications, including Chantix (prescribed for those who are trying to quit smoking) and some beta-blockers, used to treat heart disease, have depression listed as a possible side effect.

☞ REALITY CHECK

So what is depression? Generally speaking, it's the feeling that there is no point to living. The good news, however, is that depression is a medical condition that can be treated.

1. You can't "snap out" of depression. It's not all in your head. It's a physical condition for which treatment is available.

2. If you or someone you care about has been experiencing symptoms of depression for more than two weeks, it's time to see the doctor.

3. There is treatment available. Sometimes, treating your depressed state is as simple as changing prescription medications. For medical conditions for which depression is a symptom, prescription medications are available. Check with your doctor, and be sure to bring all the medications you're currently using for the doctor to evaluate. Sometimes, medications can interact with negative, even life-threatening side effects.

4. One last thought on depression. Research has found that the onset of depression in men who have never been diagnosed with depression previously may be a symptom of an impending heart attack. If this describes you or someone you know, seek medical intervention immediately.[33]

Of all the issues we tackle as we age, our health is probably our number one priority. Our respondents thought about this a lot, and so have we. Unlike at other times in our lives, our later years are when we are forced to realize the impact that lifelong choices have made on our bodies and minds. If we overeat, overdrink, or over- or under-exercise, our bodies are quick to remind us of our bad choices, yet we're living with medical conditions today that our grandparents would have died from. We've definitely made progress, and we'll take it!

Chapter 7

RELATIONSHIPS— GETTING BETTER WITH AGE

"Treasure your relationships, not your possessions."

—ANTHONY D'ANGELO

Strong relationships foster good health, reduce stress levels, decrease depression associated with loneliness, and help us live longer. According to more than one hundred studies, people with strong social connections are 50 percent less likely to die prematurely. As a group, they even feel wealthier than people with weaker social ties. For example, a survey by the National Bureau of Economic Research found that a twofold increase in the number of friends has the same effects on well-being as increasing one's income by 50 percent.[34] No doubt, our personal relationships make a difference in our lives.[35] Perhaps surprisingly, research shows that it's older adults who have the best, most satisfying relationships of all.[36] This finding is consistent with what our respondents had to say about their own relationships.

Our respondents told us that life was easier and they were happier when they could share their joys and sorrows with someone who understood them and accepted them for who they were, regardless of their flaws and shortcomings. Some had had best friends from childhood and others had found true friendship further along in their life's journeys. They also said that relationships take work, but the work was worth it, because maintaining good relationships is essential to our health and happiness as we age. They told us that their friends were their greatest resource, and that one good friend could be a treasure.

—— IN SICKNESS AND IN HEALTH ——

For those of us who chose marriage, our spouse or partner is often our one good friend. As we age, we come to realize how precious and fragile that relationship can be.

The day we married, my new sister-in-law said, "You know, he'll never leave you." I've thought about that over the years—fifty-two years, to be exact—and she was right. And I never left him, either. We made a vow and we stuck to it, even through the roughest patches. And there were plenty of those. But we never quit. It was not an option. I wonder if young people whose marriages fail…what would happen if they decided to stick it out just one more day, one more week, until the bad times passed? Maybe too many people give up too soon.

—Eighty-year-old stuck-it-out gal

This autumn, we'll celebrate our forty-seventh anniversary. I know I haven't been the easiest guy to live with, and my wife deserves the lion's share of the credit for sticking with me. There would have been quite a few times that I wouldn't have blamed her for tossing in the towel, but she never did. She said she didn't want to go to all the trouble of breaking in a new husband, since she'd invested so much time in me. They say you get what you deserve in this life, but I don't know about that. I think fate was pretty generous to me.

—Seventy-five-year-old grateful guy

For those of our respondents who, for a variety of reasons, couldn't stick it out or for whom the challenges were just too big to ride through, divorce was common, and, as the years piled up, the death of a spouse was common as well.

I always thought I'd be the first one to go. So much cancer and heart disease in my family, I figured it was a no-brainer. Funny thing about that, though. I was just thinking about illness. I could never have prepared for my wife deciding to take her own life. I never knew she was in that kind of pain. I just never knew.

—Sixty-eight-year-old grieving widower

We always talked about taking that big trip in the RV. We were going to see every state in the continental U.S. and Alaska, too. But it never happened. One week after my husband's seventieth birthday, he died of a massive coronary. We knew it was a possibility, but it was always in the future—in some future time. It wasn't supposed to happen for a long time yet. But it did. We never took the trip. My whole world changed that day. It seems so empty now.

—Sixty-nine-year-old grieving widow

☞ REALITY CHECK

If you've been living with someone for a long time, it might be time to think about what you still find attractive about this person.

1. What do you enjoy about living with this person? What would you miss if he or she were no longer with you, because of death or a breakup?

2. What do you admire about this person?

3. Can this person still make you laugh? How?

If you look for the bad in people, you're going to find it. We're all imperfect creatures. The same goes for the good. You'll find that, too, if you look. What is it you want in your relationship? If the relationship is truly important to you, think twice before giving up on it. Maybe you'll find the good.

LOVING AGAIN

Our respondents considered several options following a divorce or the death of a spouse or partner. Some remarried, some chose to remain single, some went the cohabitation route, and others opted for separate residences with visiting privileges and without the benefits (or liabilities!) of marriage. Respondents were frank in sharing their views on love the second, third, and even fourth time around.

I've been married twice and had lovers before and between. My first marriage was young and wrong; my second was romantic and evolved into a deep friendship—the deepest of my life. I tell people my husband is my best girlfriend, and he is more my family than the one I was born into. But we've aged differently—I feel so much younger than I am, and he seems ten years older. That issue accelerated even more after his stroke a few years back. I love him dearly, but I'm suddenly married to an old man. One more passionate love affair before I die would suit me just fine! That said, I wouldn't seek it out, and doubt that I would break my marriage vows.

—Seventy-one-year-old still-romantic gal

That sentiment rang true for both our gay and straight respondents. The excerpt above is from a straight woman. The following is from a gay man.

I've been single for a long time now. I'm choosy about whom I share my time with. I've learned to enjoy the freedom of being alone, but I'm still open to finding a compatible partner. I've started relationships, but nothing has lasted very long. I let some good prospects get away in the past by not taking a risk...but I also know when to hold back or back out too. I put myself in places where I might meet somebody interesting, but I'm definitely not "desperately seeking" anyone.

—Seventy-two-year-old not-so-desperately-seeking guy

The urgency that drives romantic relationships in our younger years is noticeably absent as we mature. No longer pressed by the biological drives to reproduce, we look instead for relationships that sustain us and complement our lives more peacefully and less stressfully. Yet, in some of the responses, there was a wistfulness for the passion that was once a feature of the relationship.

I'd love to have sex one more time. It's been years, and I've almost forgotten what it feels like to be held close and loved. It would be nice, but realistically, it's probably not going to happen.

—Seventy-six-year-old wishful gal

👉 REALITY CHECK

What we want in a romantic relationship as we get older may be very different from what we wanted when we were in our twenties, thirties, and forties.

1. Whether you're married, widowed, or divorced, think for a few minutes about what's important to you in a relationship today.

2. How has what you wanted changed over the years?

3. Is your relationship with your spouse or partner providing what you need now?

4. What might you do to improve it?

GOING IT ALONE

Fifteen percent of people in the United States who are over age fifty are divorced, but unlike the figures for younger people, the rates in this group are rising, and this has created a new term: *gray divorce*.[37] The increasing lifespan of Baby Boomers, the financial security of women in this group, and changing cultural norms are all thought to contribute to this increase. Along with others in their age group, some of our respondents were divorced or no longer with their significant other. In the case of at least this one respondent, the children were not surprised when they heard the news.

You can't fool your children. You can put on your game face and try to pretend that everything's peachy keen, but they know. Maybe not when they're young, but by the time they're teenagers, they can read you better than you can read them. I finally decided it was past time to stop pretending and be free of the burden of my marriage. I wasn't going to live the last years of my life in hell. You can be much lonelier with someone who is supposed to love you and doesn't than you'll ever be by yourself.

—Sixty-five-year-old no-longer-lonely ex-wife

It may be some consolation to know, though, that once you're in your sixties or older, the chances of getting divorced are as low as 4 percent.[38] If you're still married, you're likely to stay that way.

☞ REALITY CHECK

Nothing lasts forever. Not the good, not the bad, not the joy, and not the pain. It may help to remind yourself that you have little or no control over the decisions others make. All you can do is your best in any situation, so practice forgiving yourself for your humanness and forgiving others for theirs.

1. If you're divorced, do you regret that it

> happened? What, if anything, could you have possibly done to prevent it?
>
> 2. If you're still married, what's the secret to your success? What tips might you give others for a long and successful marriage?

SIBLINGS: THE TIES THAT BIND

You may be lucky enough to consider your spouse or partner your best friend, but if you're like many older people, a brother or sister may have that honor or be a close second. It should come as no surprise that our relationships with our siblings are among the most intense and influential we ever have.[39] After all, we share DNA and a strong biological connection with them.

For many of us, our siblings are our first peers, helping to shape our social skills and ways of interacting with others. As we spent time with them as children and teenagers, we learned with them and from them about power, sharing, conflict management, kindness, and other aspects of interacting that can be useful throughout our lives. In short, our siblings, if we had them, were extremely instrumental in shaping our relationships with friends, coworkers, and romantic partners.

As some of our respondents told us, our siblings are also important in shaping our sense of who we are, our identities.

I love my older sister. As I've become an "elder" and look back over my life, I see how influential she was to the person I became. I can see how, in part, I am what I am because of what she was or wasn't. We both loved sports, but my parents seemed to think my sister was gifted and I just worked hard; that was why I was good. My sister was very gregarious; thus, relatively speaking, I became the quiet, shy, somber one in my parents' eyes. I never really thought I was shy or somber, but I can see how they must have thought that, given my sister's more gregarious nature. I thought I seemed pretty normal. I can see how immensely my parents' perception of my sister influenced how I thought about myself. I became the hard worker; my sister was the one with the natural talent. I would often hear my parents tell this to their friends and other family members; thus, I came to believe it was true. Unlike today, when women are in every sport imaginable, there weren't many oppor-tunities for my sister to participate in sports when we were young, so she never really got to test the "innate ability" my parents thought she had, but I still knew that they believed my sister should have been the athlete in our family. While I had some successes in high school, I always felt a bit insecure about my abilities and never quite had the confi-dence that my sister seems to have about life. I can still hear my parents' voice in my mind as they would comment that my sister was the one with the real "talent." I can see now how their perception of my ability had a huge influence on my confidence throughout my life.

—Seventy-three-year-old working-harder athlete

My brother used to help me with my algebra when I was young. He hated to do it and often wasn't too nice about having to help me. My parents made him do it. They always thought he was the smart one in the family, and you know, he really was. It wasn't that I was dumb or anything; he just had a real knack for math. Today, we have some great laughs about our parents making him help me. We both agree that it did more harm than good for our relationship.

—Sixty-seven-year-old
needed-help-with-his-math brother

In some families, these labels clearly influence future behavior by defining us as *good, bad,* or, as this respondent recalled, *the troublemaker.*

My brother was always getting in trouble. I was the good one in the family. I remember thinking my parents were pretty hard on him, and maybe that's why he acted out so much. He died a few years ago of alcoholism. I loved him dearly, but early on he was labeled the troublemaker and I was labeled the good girl. I can see today how both my brother and I played out the labels our parents gave us. I don't think he was so bad; it's just that I rarely did anything my parents didn't want me to do, so he didn't have a chance. I'm sure my parents didn't mean to, but my brother just lived up to the expectations they had for him.

—Sixty-nine-year-old good girl

As research shows us, and as you've probably noticed, parents label their children relative to their siblings. If you got better grades than your sibling (regardless of how much better), you were probably labeled the *smart* one, while your siblings may not have gotten credit even if they were just as smart. If a sibling is hugely financially successful as an adult, regardless of how well you have done for yourself, she's likely to be forever labeled as the *success* in the family and you as less successful.

The suggestion seems to be—and research supports this—that there's room for only one *smart, athletic,* or *creative* child in each family. Whoever is the first to garner the label of *good kid, smart kid, athlete, musically inclined, nice one, thoughtful one,* and so on is given that label, while the other siblings, at least with respect to that label, are always defined as not quite measuring up. You may have been a great athlete, musician, or mathematician, but if one of your siblings happened to be even a bit better, you were more than likely labeled as *less than* in this category.

—————— **MOM AND DAD ALWAYS** ——————
LIKED HIM BEST

The strongest influence on whether the relationship between siblings is healthy or flawed is, as one might expect, the parents' relationships with their children and their interactions with each other. Alix Spiegel, in an article about sibling relationships, reported on a Purdue University study that found that if a child thought her parents showed favoritism toward her or one of her siblings, she felt less loved by the sibling. Surprisingly, whether the child was the favorite or not didn't affect the findings. It was the perception of favoritism that affected whether the child felt her sibling loved her.

As Spiegel also noted, mood, health, morale, stress, and life satisfaction, among other aspects of our lives as adults, are all influenced by our relationship with our siblings.[40] In families in which there is little to no favoritism, the chances are much better that the relationships among siblings will be positive and loving as they grow up and get older. We were pleased to hear from respondents like this one whose parents must have done something right!

My parents always made me and my siblings feel like we were the favored one. I would hear other people say that their parents liked one or the other of their siblings the best, but my parents made us all feel like we were the favored one. I always thought this was why we all turned out so emotionally and psychological strong. We never felt competition between each other and always knew our parents loved us all the "best."

—Seventy-year-old mom-and-dad-love-her-best gal

Research suggests that even into old age, positive contact with our siblings enhances our mood and helps us feel more loved and less lonely. Spiegel reports on a Swedish study that shows that even in our eighties, positive contact with our siblings can be more important than our relationships with friends or adult children. In this study, whether the sibling was receiving or providing the support didn't matter; the act of being in contact eased loneliness.[41] As one of our respondents told us, the power of the brother–sister bond can be tremendous.

My brother sent me a text the other day that said, "I just realized I hadn't told you how much I love you in a while so here it is...I love you." My husband doesn't do that...

my kids don't do that…my friends don't do that—just my brother does that. Makes me smile!

—Seventy-year-old brother-makes-her-smile gal

The best gift our parents ever gave us was our brothers and sisters. They never asked us to be best friends or forced us to spend time with each other. But they showed us through their own loving ways toward each other, their relationship with their own parents and siblings and each of us, that family is the best and strongest relationship we will ever have. To this day, my favorite phone call, text, or email is the one from one of my siblings. I can't even think of what my life will be like when one of them is gone.

—Eighty-one-year-old not-going-to-think-about-it sib

SIBLING CONFLICTS

As with any important relationship, the one among siblings can become challenged by rivalries or conflicts. Decisions about how to care for elderly parents can be especially difficult and fuel competition for attention and power as well as resurface unresolved rivalries and jealousies. Conflicts over who is in charge of providing or paying for the care can also cause tension, even between siblings who have historically gotten along well. Factor in the sadness adult children are likely to feel if their parents are in poor health, and you can see how easily the sibling relationship can become frayed, as one respondent heartbreakingly described.[42]

> *My siblings don't live near our parents and I do, or did, as they are now gone. I did everything for my parents while my siblings just stood by and watched. While one of my sisters lives in a different state, my brother is right here in the same location and could have easily been more help. It's very hard not to feel resentful that the responsibility fell on my shoulders just because I lived near them. I don't think any of them have any idea how difficult it was on me and my immediate family. My husband was a trooper, but for a long, long time there was a lot of friction between us because of the challenging responsibility that we alone faced. I could hardly speak to any of my siblings at the funeral—they could have done much more and they know it! I'm not sure I will ever forgive them.*
>
> —Sixty-six-year-old still-resentful sis

As we heard from another of our respondents, in some cases, siblings can handle such situations maturely and avoid painful feuding.

I'm eternally grateful that my brother cared for both my mom and dad as they became elderly and too ill to care for themselves. He never made the rest of us feel guilty for not being there, yet we all knew it must have taken a terrible physical and emotional toll on him and his wife. The rest of us tried to do what we could, but our older brother had the lion's share of the responsibility for them. When it came time to divvy up some of their prized possessions, the rest of us all agreed that our brother and sister-in-law should get to choose anything they wanted.

—Sixty-five-year-old grateful brother

Like all relationships, those among adult siblings run the continuum from great to poor, with variations throughout the lives of the siblings. We often hear about misunderstandings, estrangement, and jealousies, and these are all too common; yet, as the research bears out and our respondents attest, it's a relationship worth nurturing and cherishing.

☞ REALITY CHECK

You may give little thought to your relationship with your siblings, especially now that you're older. Understanding it better may prove valuable, however, in helping you better understand yourself and the values you were given as a child.

1. What labels were you given as a child (e.g., the smart one, the athletic one, the musical one)? How do you think the labels affected your relationship with your siblings?

2. How have you and your siblings handled family crises? Did you resort to roles and behaviors you developed as children? What might you have done differently to better handle difficult situations?

3. What specific actions would make your relationship with a brother or sister better (e.g., call, email, or text more frequently; remember birthdays or anniversaries; involve the sibling in celebrations with your immediate family)?

4. If you're an only child, have you ever thought about what you missed out on by not having a sibling? If so, how? In what ways is your situation easier or harder than if you had a sibling?

THE MOST WONDERFUL RELATIONSHIP OF ALL

"Grandchildren are God's way of compensating us for growing old."

—MARY H. WALDRIN

They aren't ours...we know, we get that. In her book *Eye of My Heart*, Barbara Graham describes when her first granddaughter, Isabelle, was born. She noted, "She was mine but not mine." That explains how many grandparents feel about their grandchildren. Whatever the limitations, though, for many of us, becoming a grandparent is one of the very best things that *ever* happens to us.[43] Most of our respondents felt this way.

There are so many wonderful moments, but one I'll never forget is a call I got from my five-year-old grandson. "Nania," he said, "tomorrow is Bring Your Favorite Thing to School Day, and you are my favorite thing. Can you come?" I've always thought his mom might have put him up to this, but it didn't matter. I've never been prouder than that day when I sat on the little kindergarten chair in the corner of the room, with all the other favorite things—basketballs, dolls, trucks, blankets, and waited my turn to be presented to the class by my grandson. I wasn't the only one crying. The teacher couldn't hold back her tears either as he placed his arm around my shoulder and gave his presentation about me, noting that I was a professor, had traveled all over the world, had moved to California so I could be near him. He ended his presentation by saying, "She used to be a professor, but now she's just my grandma." I tell this story a lot. When I do, I can never make it through without shedding a bunch of happy tears.

—Seventy-year-old "just a grandma now"

One of my favorite moments ever was with my grandson when I took him to the library for the first time. He was probably about three years old. We walked to the library to get him his very first library card. He could barely reach the top of the librarian's desk when he said to her, "May I get a libary card?" So many times when I'm with him I can hardly hold back my tears—I'm so proud, so touched, and so in love with him. We got his first libary card, and he's never forgotten the experience. He loves to read and is the smartest kid in the class (I always wonder how all of my friends and I can each have the smartest kid in the class, yet I never question the label).

—Seventy-year-old grandma
with the smartest kid in the class

Many of our respondents regaled us about the joys of being a grandparent, how wonderful it is to have a child you can love but for whom you're not responsible; someone who won't blame you for their problems as they get older; someone you don't have to make eat their vegetables, take their vitamins, or do their homework. Someone, many said, who you can just give cupcakes and lots of hugs to.

Vikki Claflin puts a humorous spin on the differences between parenting and grandparenting on the popular website *Scary Mommy*:

Parenting is hard. It's basically 18 years of schooling an often-recalcitrant young human into how to be a socially acceptable, productive member of the community. Grandparenting, however, is less goal-oriented. We are not actually raising the future of our country. When little Johnny sets the neighbor's doghouse on fire or young Sally rides home on the back of her new boyfriend's Harley, proudly wearing his dirty leather jacket emblazoned with an oversize "Road Kill" back patch, nobody asks, "Where are the grandparents?"[44]

SO, WHAT'S MY ROLE?

Grandparents have always played a significant role in the lives of their grandchildren, and grandparents continue to have a major role today, not the least as important caregivers. One study found that 21 percent of all children ages five and under are cared for by grandparents in some way, and that figure appears to be rising.[45]

It is not uncommon in families in which both parents work, the mother or father is a single parent, or one or both parents are disabled or incarcerated, for a grandparent to be a child's primary caregiver for many hours each day, if not 24/7. There are bound to be challenges in the parent–adult child and grandparent–grandchild relationships given these circumstances, especially as the grandparents face the physical problems of aging.

In other families, the grandparents provide care only occasionally by giving the parents welcome time to enjoy themselves, temporarily free from parental responsibilities. Other grandparents appear only for the fun times, and still others don't want to be involved in the grandchildren's lives at all.

Regardless of the relationship, the transition to grand-parenting is different for each of us. A few respondents we spoke with were less than eager to take on the role, saying that it reminded them too much that they were *old*. Others had had enough of the "childcare thing" and had no interest in being part of raising any more children. The vast majority of respondents we talked to, though, thought that being a grandparent was one of the best things that had ever happened to them. For many who hadn't had a great relationship with their children, it felt like a second chance, and they approached grandparenting with an open and hopeful heart.

I was never one of those people who believed in love at first sight. That was, until my granddaughter, Brynn, was born.

—Sixty-seven-year-old in-love-at-first-sight grandma

I've never felt more peaceful, serene, or hopeful than when my grandson was born. He was our first grandchild. Seriously, he can do no wrong. It's such an odd phenomenon because I felt so bonded with him immediately, yet there was this wall that needed to be penetrated to reach him (his parents). I'm lucky my daughter and son-in-law are so generous with their children and value the importance of a grandparent to a grandchild.

—Seventy-seven-year-old
broke-down-the-walls grandma

I guess I never had time to do it with my own kids, but I take my grandsons on a monthlong fishing, hiking, or camping trip every summer. We rarely shower, eat whatever we want, and have the best time I've ever had in my life.

—Seventy-five-year-old

not-making-them-shower grandpa

Almost all the grandparents we heard from agreed that they were not parenting as they'd done with their own children. As parents, they sometimes had to be strict, maintain a long-term perspective, and have goals for their children. As grandparents, they got to enjoy being in the moment, not judging, not making demands, setting fewer expectations. Many had thought their own kids were works in progress. By contrast, their grandchildren were perfect just the way they were.

By the time we're grandparents, most of us have learned to loosen up a bit. We realize that we may have made some mistakes with our own children, that it's too late to change anything, and the outcomes were fine regardless. We now realize that some aspects of parenting are simply out of our control. The attitude with our grandchildren is that there's no point in wasting precious time with worry. Nope…we're just going to enjoy being with them.

Our respondents repeated many times that the benefits of being a grandparent were numerous. But what about the benefits for the child? Research confirms that the benefits for the child are also significant. A nurturing, healthy relationship with grandparents can have a huge impact on a child's development.[46] Grandparents can be models of unconditional love. They can be sources of wisdom grounded in years of experience. And they can be fun playmates who have the time to enjoy activities with children whose parents may not have time. Is it any wonder that anthropologist Margaret Mead once observed that "the closest friends I have made all through life have been people who grew up close to a loved and loving grandmother or grandfather."[47]

One other benefit of being a grandparent that our respondents mentioned is that grandchildren provide a link to the future and a sense of continuity, reminding us that we will live on through them. So maybe one of the best things about being a grandparent is that it reminds us all that we'll live on through our children and grandchildren.

Grandkids give you a renewed purpose of life.

—Seventy-one-year-old

got-a-new-purpose-in-life grandpa

My granddaughter reminds me so much of my daughter. It's both beautiful and heartbreaking to watch. The love is so much more uncontrollable being a grandpa. Being a parent, I felt the love all right, but I think I mostly felt I wanted to protect my daughter, teach her ways to learn to protect herself, help her be the very best human being she could ever be. As a grandparent, I just want to accept my granddaughter, love her, and not judge her ever. Why would I? She's so perfect just the way she is.

—Seventy-three-year-old
thinking-she's-just-perfect grandpa

I've always been so close to my daughter. I couldn't ever imagine loving anyone more than her, but then up popped my granddaughter, Sophia.

—Seventy-nine-year-old
loving-his-granddaughter grandpa

It doesn't have to be something special; I love even just picking them up from school.

—Seventy-year-old
doesn't-have-to-be-special grandma

👉 REALITY CHECK

1. If you're a grandparent, think for a moment about your relationship with your grand-children. How is it different from the relation-ship you had with your own children?

2. What might you consider doing to make your relationship with your grandchildren stronger? What, if anything, is standing in your way?

3. What, if any, relationship did your children have with their grandparents? How did it help shape who they are today and the role they want you to play in their children's (your grandchildren's) lives?

4. How did your grandparents' behaviors affect how you treat your own grandchildren?

YOU'RE NEVER TOO OLD TO MAKE NEW FRIENDS

In addition to their relationships with their spouses, partners, siblings, and grandchildren, our respondents emphasized the value of their platonic friendships. They may have fewer friends than when they were younger, but the depth and strength of these relationships were powerful in helping ward off loneliness and depression, resulting in improved health and cognitive functioning.

> *I've got four close friends and numerous acquaintances—not close friends, but close enough. There's been a lot of attrition, to be sure. I don't bother with high school reunions. All my friends from back then are dead. Makes you wonder why them and not me, but I keep a few friends close. They listen to my troubles, and I listen to theirs. If you're really lucky, you'll be blessed with a few truly good friends.*
>
> —Seventy-seven-year-old gal with four good friends

> *When I get together with my girlfriends—we've known each other since our graduate school days, back in Columbus, Ohio, in 1969—we've got a favorite saying: "It takes three of us to get one of us out the door." It seems that there's just so much to remember: glasses, keys, sweater, shopping list, whatever. Definitely too much for one person to handle, but with three, it works out fine. These gals are closer to me and understand me better than my sister.*
>
> —Seventy-year-old out-the-door woman

> *I've got a buddy—we've been friends for, I don't know, maybe forty, forty-five years. We don't talk all that often, but if I*

ever get in a jam, I can count on him. He'd be here if I asked him to be. No questions asked. And the same goes for me. He knows that, but we don't talk about it. It's just the way it is.

—Seventy-six-year-old true friend

Several of our respondents noted how surprised they were that they had made some of their closest friends in their later years. They considered it one of the very best aspects of growing older.

I moved to a new state when I was sixty years old. I met one of the very best friends I have ever known in my entire life. I never even gave it a thought that I would find such a friend. We don't really have a lot in common; we grew up in entirely different environments, have very different educational backgrounds and work experiences. I'm not sure we would have been friends if we had met earlier in our lives. But at this time in our lives, we are just perfect for each other. I've never been one to share much of my life with others, but I can tell her anything, and I know it will go nowhere. I've never had a friend that I have trusted so much. What a treat to have such a friend at this time in my life, when life gets more challenging, when I need a friend just like her.

—Seventy-year-old loving-her-new-friend gal

There are three of us. We all met in the later years of our lives. We call ourselves sisters, because that's just how we think of each other. We have some disagreements just like real sisters, and we compete like real sisters, but just let someone try to criticize one of us and we are stuck like glue. We don't have to be doing anything fancy to have a good time. Our favorite times are at our "sister meetings," which is code for having a glass of wine and laughing our asses off like we were sixteen again. We often claim we can't believe we have been so lucky to have met each other in what most might describe as a very random way.

—Seventy-one-year-old with two sisters now

As at least one respondent told us that even though you may be old, your friends don't have to be.

I never gave it much thought before, but my friends are different ages. What I mean is, I have a friend who's fifteen years younger than I am. We both like to quilt, and we met at our quilt guild. We go out to lunch and hit the thrift stores and have a wonderful time. And then there's my other friend who's twelve years older than I am. We met at a writer's conference. We also love to go out to lunch and chat. Limiting your friends to people who are your age is really limiting. When we're together we don't focus on age but on our interests. It's nice.

—Seventy-year-old bridging-the-age-gap gal

☞ REALITY CHECK

It can be scary to reach out to someone new, but forging new friendships is one of the best ways to keep yourself feeling young and engaged. Plus, it's just plain fun! Here are some things to think about as you discover ways to make new friends.

1. Have you made any new friends in your later years?

2. How are these friendships different from friendships you had when you were younger?

3. What are you looking for in your friendships now?

4. Has what you wanted in your friendships changed since you were younger?

We hope this chapter has reinforced your notion of the importance of relationships to living happy, healthy, and longer lives and will help you remember the importance of growing and maintaining those relationships. Taking time to evaluate your relationships can help you better appreciate your friends and significant others and all they bring to your lives. There's no better time than the present to let these people know what they mean to you, and no better time to renew old friendships that you may have let lapse.

Chapter 8

FAITH, RELIGION, AND SPIRITUALITY

Our Invisible Means of Support

"It's time to ask yourself what you believe."

—Walter Donovan to Indiana Jones in
Indiana Jones and the Last Crusade

In chapter 7, we looked at relationships—the connections we have with others. This chapter concerns itself with the most intimate relationship of all: our connection with who we are at our core and how we understand our place and our role in this life, and, depending on our perspective, what may come after this life has run its earthly course. We took the quote that begins this chapter to heart and asked ourselves and hundreds of other people: "What do you believe?" Then, we asked if these beliefs had changed or remained the same over the years. If they had changed, we wanted to know why and in what ways.

Religion, faith, spirituality. Whichever of these guides our lives and our decision-making, it is a response to a need inherent in our species—to comprehend the unknowable—and addresses that need in a way that makes sense to each individual. Defining our terms for this chapter ranged from simple (religion) to nearly impossible (spirituality).

— FINDING THE RIGHT RELIGIOUS FIT —

"You have to believe in gods to see them."

—HOPI INDIAN SAYING

Religion is fairly easily defined. It comes from the Latin verb *religio,* which means *to bind together.* So, religion is essentially an organized set of beliefs with a membership that adheres (to varying degrees) to those beliefs. *The Merck Manual* reports that people sixty-five years of age and older comprise the most actively religious demographic in the United States. Ninety-six percent of these adherents believe in God or a universal spirit, more than 90 percent pray, and more than 50 percent attend a weekly religious service.[48] The reasons for their engagement with religion are many and complex. Apart from the basic function of providing a spiritual home, religious organizations are essentially social in nature. They provide emotional support, care for physical needs, and provide opportunities for socializing and volunteering. These functions become increasingly important as we grow older and find our youthful independence and good health eroding. It's inevitable, then, that at some point we will need to rely more and more on others, and often our religious choices fill that need, putting us in close contact with like-minded people who are oriented toward helping others within their community. It's true that there's safety in numbers. If everyone around you is a like thinker, you are affirmed.

My church is my home. It's my link to my friends—the people who think the way I do. We have meetings apart from the religious service. It's where my bridge club meets.
                    —Ninety-two-year-old bridge player

We go to church every weekend and feel it's good to pray. I think it's important to belong to a religious group, even if you just go once a week.
                    —Eighty-four-year-old with priorities

Faith in the love of God, through his son, Jesus Christ, is the determining factor in how I face life, death, and aging. As an ex-police officer who has dealt with death frequently at

all ages, I would hope to be a better witness for my Savior,
Jesus Christ. As a minister of the gospel to older Christians, I
have never heard a dying person say they wish they had done
less for the cause of Christ, but I have heard many say they
regretted not doing more.

—Seventy-one-year-old Baptist minister

——— FINDING THE PERFECT FIT ———

Some religions tolerate a certain degree of independent thinking among their members; others do not. It's probably for this
reason that people who didn't follow any particular religion
were labeled *freethinkers* in times past. Some of our respondents
had once been members of a religious group, but instead of
experiencing support and acceptance through this association,
they were shunned because their lifestyles didn't mesh with
what was acceptable to the congregation or they voiced opposi-
tion to the group's social or political activism. Consequently,
they left religion behind, or as some shared with us, their
churches abandoned them.

I'm a little hesitant to relate this, but life has been far
more difficult and painful than I ever dreamed, in spite of
growing up in an extremely dysfunctional family. I guess

I thought I could do a better job than my parents did, and in some ways I have, but it has been costly spiritually. I have evolved from being a Christian as a child and teenager to being at least agnostic if not atheistic now. Somehow it strikes me as having been the meanest fairy tale of all. The finishing touches were put on this evolution by a number of mainstream Christian denominations over a fifty-year span, all of whom were very rejecting of my gay son, even as a young boy, and of me in the role of his mother, my most favorite role of all. He and his partner were the loves of my life. His partner died eighteen years ago, and my son died thirteen years ago, both due to complications of AIDS. There simply was no compassion or support from the religious community. Thankfully, I was working with a local AIDS support group and AIDS task force headed by our local public health department, and those people were the ones who, unknowingly to them then, helped me keep it together. These were the two losses of many that I will never recover from. The brick wall of hatred from the religious communities here was unbelievable. I survived, but I will never return to organized religion. I'm sorry for the downer, but it's always on my mind in one way or another.

—Seventy-six-year-old mother with deep regret

For others, familiar religious rituals bring comfort, but they no longer believe their religion has all the answers.

I have a very strong set of moral values and hate that the world is going to hell in a handbasket. I attend Mass regularly and do a lot of praying. Lately, I find myself asking more questions than I used to, and I believe aging brings this to the forefront.

—Seventy-year-old questioner

Some of our respondents were angry at God, fate, or karma.

Don't tell me there's a God. If there were, there wouldn't be so much evil and suffering in the world. There's no reason for it. Where was God when my child died?

—Seventy-three-year-old with a bitter taste in her mouth

☞ **REALITY CHECK**

"I have not lost faith in God. I have moments of anger and protest. Sometimes I've been closer to Him for that reason."

—ALBERT CAMUS

It may be helpful to remember that religions are organizations of people; some of these people are good and kind, others are not. If one religion has let you down and you feel the need to belong to a group of people who think as you do, know that there are more than 2,400 religions worldwide. One of these may be the perfect fit for you.

1. Have you ever felt anger at God or fate or karma? How did you resolve that anger?

2. Are you comfortable talking about your belief system with others?

3. How have your beliefs changed over the course of your lifetime? What circumstances caused these changes?

4. Have you arrived at a belief system that you are comfortable with and secure in? If not, how are you continuing your journey to find the answers you seek?

5. Would conversations with friends help you sort out the issues?

——————— **UNDERSTANDING FAITH** ———————

Faith is the belief in that which cannot be seen. It's an integral part of religion and can be a component of spirituality affiliated with a religion. Faith is confidence that all is somehow working toward the greater good. For those who have faith in God, in a higher power, or in the eventual triumph of good over evil, the answers can wait and some of our respondents are comfortable not having their questions answered now.

> *My faith is primary in my life and always has been. The Lord has blessed me, and I give Him the glory. He is my Savior, my friend, my creator, my redeemer. He has seen me through good times, and He has seen me through bad times. Because He is always there, I know that I can handle any situation.*
>
> —Sixty-nine-year-old believer

> *If you've taken care to lay a strong faith foundation, then that aspect of your life only grows stronger with age.*
>
> —Seventy-six-year-old with a strong foundation

> *I'm a Jew, but I guess you'd have to call me a cultural Jew. I've never been particularly observant, but given that, I'm a*

Jew. Do I believe in hell? No. But I entertain the possibility
of heaven. Why not? What's to lose?

—Eighty-two-year-old with an open mind

——— SEEKING SPIRITUALITY ———

Defining spirituality turned out to be similar to defining
art. Essentially, it's in the eye of the beholder. Those of our
respondents who chose spirituality as their core were quite
clear as to what it meant to them individually. There seemed
to be as many variations of spirituality as there were denominations of religion.

I am not big on formal religion but do enjoy my own spiritu-
ality. The yoga sessions I attend and my meditation routines
are important aspects of my life. I am annoyed when others
make attempts to push their organized religious beliefs,
including the Tea Party politicians.

—Sixty-five-year-old yoga practitioner

I believe more in spirituality than being a person that has to
go to church just so I can say I have faith. I do believe in a
supreme being, and I know that God is with me.

—Seventy-five-year-old confident freethinker

My spiritual life took off in my mid-fifties. It has a profound impact on my life. I belong to the Unity Church, which is more spiritual than religious. It's helped me cope to be a more positive person and give back to my community. I read somewhere you should live your life the way you'd want your eulogy to read. What's your eulogy? You want people to say, "She really made a difference in my life. She helped me put things in perspective."

—Eighty-six-year-old Unitarian

CHART YOUR OWN PATH

For many of our respondents, their faith was their anchor in times of stress, grief, and joy. It gave meaning to life and the hope of something beyond this life. For others, religion was less important than spirituality, and they were quite clear in the differences. And still others challenged the very necessity of a belief in a higher power.

Perhaps more than any other identifier, faith, religion, and spirituality speak to who we are. If our parents were religious, our indoctrination began at birth and continued throughout our formative years. When we reached the age of questioning, religion came in for its fair share of examination. Some of us kept the faith of our youth, while others sought new ways to answer the eternal questions: "Who am I?" "Why am I here?" "Where am I going?"

I've learned to relax a bit, as I've gotten older. At some point I realized I wasn't in charge, and that freed me up to let things go. I don't need to know all the answers. I guess that's a kind of wisdom, if you're open to accepting your place in the greater scheme of things. My faith sustains me.

—Eighty-seven-year-old who's learned to relax

I used to be Catholic. I suppose I still am in some sense. They say, "Once a Catholic, always a Catholic," but I think differently now than I used to. Nobody knows any more about God than I do. I don't mean to sound egotistical, but really. How can anybody know the unknowable? My church is nature. My sacraments are the blessings I receive when I gaze upon the infinity of the night sky.

—Seventy-year-old former Catholic

And for some respondents, ethics and morality were not tied to any specific core group of beliefs or practices.

Traditional organized religion is good for many things, but unfortunately, like the institution of marriage (which is

one of its mainstays), it's abused or twisted into something
bad too often, in my opinion. And most of the good people
at a church, synagogue, temple, or mosque are just going
through the motions. They don't "live" their faith. I think
I do.

I believe in one of Unity School of Religion's foundation
teachings: "Thoughts held in mind produce in kind."

—Seventy-four-year-old Unitarian

Others took solace in the belief that the universe was
unfolding as it should.

Let's be honest. No one knows what happens when our
bodies stop working. I'm not worried about it. I've been a
casual churchgoer and even a born-again Christian. I live a
decent life, doing unto others as I want them to do unto me,
as I was taught. Today, I pick up different parts of religions
that work for me, like from a smorgasbord. I embrace more
of Eastern religion and the spirituality of indigenous peoples
in America than Christianity. In Buddhism, one of the noble
truths is that life is hard, and once you accept that, it's not
quite so hard. That, along with charity and respect for all
life, works best for me now.

—Seventy-eight-year-old decent person

One thing became clear as we spoke with our respondents: everyone had given serious and prolonged thought to the importance of religion or spirituality in their lives. Arriving at a final decision was the culmination of a lifetime of experiences, both good and bad. It seemed that life itself was the catalyst, and faith, religion, and spirituality the end products of the experiment.

The universe is bigger and more powerful than anything our limited intelligence can create. We have such ego. It's hard to admit that we have no control over so much in this life. Why not live it the best we can, and then when it's time to leave, leave it the best we can, as well. When I depart, I want people to muse, "Off he goes into the wild blue yonder."
—Ninety-three-year-old with wings

Older adults are believers, skeptics, and other-thinkers. Research tells us that people who believe in *something*—a power greater than themselves—live longer and are healthier than those who have no such beliefs.[49] Perhaps at the crux of this is the social dimension, especially as mobility decreases, along with the ability to access other, more physical outlets, and the benefits of a faith system become more essential to health and well-being. Isolation and depression are serious issues among the elderly, and to help combat this, many religious groups offer transportation to their older members so that they can attend religious services and social functions at their churches, temples, mosques, or synagogues.

Faith, religion, and spirituality give us something to lean on when we need support. They give us strength to face pain, loss, and the unknown.

Whatever belief system supports you on your journey through life, it's likely the right one for you. If we learned anything from our respondents, it's that faith, religion, and spirituality are intensely individual. There are skeptics among us, as well as staunch believers. Each person is unique, and so is the journey.

Did our respondents' beliefs change as they aged? In some cases, yes, and in others, no. It didn't seem to matter what hardships or losses they faced. If they were comfortable in their beliefs, they felt supported. If they did not experience support from their religious affiliation, they felt betrayed, isolated, and confused. Many of these former believers sought other avenues to give them solace and a sense of purpose.

The search for the answers to life's questions and problems is common to the human experience. Of all the creatures on Earth, we are the only ones who ask "Why?" For some, faith, religion, and spirituality provide the answers. For others, the search continues.

Chapter 9

LOSS: GOODBYE IS THE SADDEST WORD OF ALL

"How lucky I am to have something that makes saying goodbye so hard."

—WINNIE-THE-POOH

Growing older brings challenges, to be sure, and our respondents faced their share of challenges to their health, their independence, and their sense of well-being. Perhaps the most difficult of these challenges, however, was dealing with loss.

We've all experienced loss in one form or another—a job, a group of friends after college, a child who moved away or got married. As we get older, we may mourn the loss of a dream—becoming a world-class pianist, solving world hunger, finding a cure for cancer. Our respondents clearly felt, however, that one loss hurts more than the others: losing someone we love, whether a close friend, family member, or a spouse or partner.

Sometimes, the loss comes after an extended illness.

My wife had a stroke ten years ago. She died this spring. I know many of my friends think I feel relief, but I don't— not at all. I miss her. I loved caring for her, she continued to be my companion until the end. Sure, our life wasn't what it used to be, and I know our friends often felt sorry for me, but we were best friends until her last breath. I don't feel relief at all. I just feel a terrible void in my life.

—Seventy-nine-year-old feeling-a-void guy

I wish I could just have her back for a day, an hour, a moment. There is so much I still need to tell her.

—Seventy-one-year-old who misses his wife

Sometimes, the loss comes as a shock.

In our church, a man came to worship with his family and praised God openly with hands and heart. It was his son's ninth birthday and they had a party planned that afternoon. When his wife went to the barn to get him to prepare for the party, he was dead by hanging. His wife and three children moved into her parents' home and have remained there for over a year. Her parents have indicated they want to help

*them move forward but this delicate situation seems impos-
sible. This family seems paralyzed.*

—Seventy-year-old helpless-in-Ohio friend

*I had lost other people in the past: my brother, my uncle, a
neighbor I'd known for over thirty years. I remember being
really sad for a long time and I would think of them often.
But nothing, nothing at all, even begins to touch the sadness
I have felt from losing my husband of nearly fifty years. It
was a freak accident as he was walking home one night.
There was no warning. He was healthy as could be. We had
plans, lots of plans. We did everything together and were so
enjoying our retirement. Everybody loved him. He was the
life of every party. Now, I can't imagine going through the
rest of my life without him.*

—Seventy-nine-year-old sad widow

Coping with loss is perhaps the most difficult ordeal we can
experience, and for that reason, some writers try to spin loss as
a potentially positive experience. They claim that dealing with
loss is an *art*, something that helps us grow, learn about who
we are, and become stronger and better people. In her book
Necessary Losses, for example, Judith Viorst proposes that
the way we react to loss and our experience with it is a huge

indicator of the people we will become: "It is only through our losses that we become fully developed human beings."[50]

Most of us, though, would rather be less strong, less fully developed than we could be, and have the ones we love still with us. We may try to remember the last words we said to him or her and hope they were kind. We wonder: *Where did I last see her? Was there more I should have done for him? I hope she knows I loved her. Did I tell him enough?*

Some of our respondents were painfully blunt when discussing this topic.

From my experience with my husband's death, I have trouble letting him be dead. I move him from heaven to hell over and over. Thankfully, I didn't have anything to do with his eternal destiny. Even though our relationship was vastly flawed, his death rocked my world and that of our adult children. Yes, I agree that eventually this loss will mold me into a stronger, better human. The amount of time this takes is dependent on factors like faith, support, encouragement, resolve, and mental, emotional health of individuals. Loss sucks but the reality is death is final. No amount of grief, suffering, or denial will change the fact that he is gone. At some point the one left with the loss must cope. The loss can't dictate your entire life forever. For a family, someone must be a hero here,

too. It could be giving everyone permission to feel remorse,
then permission to move forward in a healthy way.

—Sixty-nine-year-old grieving spouse

EXPERIENCE THE PAIN

The pain we feel upon the death of a loved one is devastating. The feelings can run the gamut of shock, guilt, fear, anger, despair, sadness, and occasionally relief. The emotions may take us by surprise and last for a day, a week, or much, much longer, especially when a death is sudden or tragic.

According to psychiatrist Elisabeth Kübler-Ross, grief after the death of a loved one encompasses five stages: denial, anger, bargaining, depression, and acceptance.[51] Not everyone experiences these stages in the same way or the same order, or at all. Typically, during the denial stage, we are in disbelief that the loss has occurred. We may feel anger as we question why the loss happened and who is to blame. During the bargaining stage, we may pray for ways to negotiate the loss away or for a compromise to diminish its intensity. During the depression stage, we fully express our sadness, before gaining acceptance, when we get on with our lives as we make peace.

How we experience loss is unique to each of us and may not follow a predictable pattern. For example, just when we think we've accepted and adapted to the loss, we may find ourselves in a puddle of tears, grieving as forcefully as when we first received the news of the loved one's death.

Lots of people say I'm strong. They couldn't have lived through the loss of their son as I did. But the truth is, sometimes I'm not so strong. I realize more every day that I'm getting old. Losing a child is worse than you can ever imagine. I'm certain it added many, many years to my age. Some days I think I can go on, that it's getting better. Then I wake up in the middle of the night sobbing, realizing I'll never see that smiling face again. I'll never again get a card from him on Mother's Day telling me how much he appreciates everything I have done for him. I'll never again receive a phone call from him asking my advice, or bragging about something good that had happened in his life. I'm really happy to have had him part of my life as long as I did, but, I'm really, really angry that it ended so soon and so tragically.

—Seventy-one-year-old still-grieving mom

PREPARE FOR THE INEVITABLE

Although we might not want to think or talk about death and dying, it's mentally and emotionally healthy to do so. As with anything else that's difficult, coping strategies will help prepare us for the losses that we know, but don't want to believe, will occur.

One of our respondents, a sixty-nine-year-old woman, summed up some of the tactics we use to avoid thinking about death and loss and why we so often avoid the topic. She also reminds us why we need to face our feelings.

I remember my dad, the most organized man I knew, trying to prepare me for his inevitable death by telling me where everything was: his will, his Medicare cards, his wishes for how he would be buried/taken care of when he died, his little safe with nothing of value in it at all. I remember being very nonchalant about it all, almost evasive. I bet he thought I didn't care, but instead, it was just too painful for me to think about for even a moment. I loved him deeply. He taught me a lot about life, and he tried to teach me about death. I just wouldn't listen.

—Sixty-nine-year-old not-so-nonchalant-now gal

STAY CONNECTED

In his book *Gratitude*, physician and best-selling author Oliver Sacks says that whenever he reaches his final moments of life, he will feel nothing but gratitude, because he will look back on his life with nothing but joy. We understand that sentiment. We may even hope we feel that same way as we are dying, but what about those who are left behind? How will they be affected by losing us? A seventy-two-year-old woman we interviewed described the terrible sadness and sense of guilt she felt as she tried to process that one of her best friends was likely dying:

> *How do we convey that every day is so precious? Just how do we send that message to our kids, grandkids? I just read an email from one of my very best friends. She now has another lump on her lung. She tries to make it sound like she's going to be OK, but I can tell from her email "voice," she's worried to death (no pun intended). I can't even explain how it made me feel. Shouldn't my first thoughts have been for her? Shouldn't my first concerns be for what I can do for her? Sure, I got there pretty quickly, but my first thought was one of immense sadness, not for her, but for me. I am really going to miss her. My circle of friends is getting smaller and smaller and smaller.*
>
> —Seventy-two-year-old feeling-sorry-for-herself woman

It was clear from our discussions and interviews that the loss of friends becomes more common as we grow older and has changed the lives of our respondents both practically and emotionally. Some realized their tennis group had started to dwindle; it was getting more difficult to form a foursome for bridge; a bowling team was getting so small that it was difficult to be in a league any longer; the Monday morning hiking group was changing and disappearing.

In many ways, we are who we are because of our close relationships and the people we have shared our lives with. As a seventy-year-old respondent told us, fear of losing our friends extends not only to those whose health is declining but also to those who are fit and youthful.

Just as I am beginning to make my breakfast, a seventy-five-year-old friend knocks on my door. He's been hiking up and down the hilliest community you may have ever seen. There isn't a bead of sweat on his forehead. It made me think I don't ever want to lose him as my friend. It makes me a bit sad to think of life without him. He's such a joy, such a great role model, such a great everything.

—Seventy-year-old who doesn't want to lose her friend

Losing close friends has been difficult for our respondents. Some were even reluctant to try to make new ones, but while it may be more difficult for older adults to make friends, our survey respondents who adapted best to their losses explained that making new friends is important. Research also confirms that those who live the longest, healthiest, most enjoyable lives have relationships that they value.[52] They have friends both old and new.

Even though it may seem hard, finding outlets to make new friends can reap lots of benefits. You may not head to the bar around the corner, as you did when you were younger, but there are other ways to make an effort to meet new people.

☞ REALITY CHECK

Some people never recover from the death of a loved one, whereas others are able to get on with their lives while still acknowledging the love and friendship they felt for the person they lost. We hope these suggestions help you prepare and cope better.

1. Having good role models helps. Who do you know who has coped with loss in a way you consider healthy? What made them a good model?

2. For some, growing old means their lives are bigger, not smaller. They are learning more than ever, and losses contribute to their

understanding of their purpose and the importance of enjoying every moment. They recognize that their life has changed, and they
embrace the change and do not fight it. Do you
know people like this? In what ways would
you like to be more like them?

3. Making new friends throughout your life is
   important. What activities might you get more
   involved in that would connect you to new
   people?

4. Your new friends don't have to look, act, or
   talk like your old friends. Make friends with
   younger people or with people whose interests
   or backgrounds are different from yours. How
   might you go about doing this?

5. Be a good role model for friends and others.
   You may help make loss less painful for them.

DEALING WITH THE MOST PAINFUL LOSSES

While psychologists debate many aspects of loss, on one thing
they agree. The loss of a spouse/partner or child is the most
difficult to bear. Our respondents wholeheartedly agreed.

Some of our respondents noted feelings of profound fear

of being left alone, in debilitating health, and unable to care for themselves; and a fearful inability to understand how life could go on without their spouse, partner, parent, or child. One sixty-five-year-old man told us about this fear in his mother.

My father died before my mother. I think he was about eighty-seven years old. My mom always seemed like the strong person in our family. My dad was ill most of his life. Mom was the major breadwinner. At the end of his funeral service, I had to walk to his open casket with my mom in front of those present. I have never seen my mom cry, and she didn't even cry that day. She just said to him in the gruff way she often spoke to him: "I can't believe you are leaving me here all by myself." While to some this may seem harsh, I knew my mom was saying the best way she could that life was going to be hard without him by her side and that she was fearful to go on without him.

—Sixty-five-year-old and still her son

I was dumbfounded when my husband died. My son said, 'Dad always acted like he was invincible, and I think I heard it so many times I believed it.' My husband used to say, 'When it gets too tough for everyone else, it's just right for me.' I found myself saying repeatedly, 'I can't believe you are not here.' But he wasn't here and never will be again. I didn't cry for months, not because I didn't feel bad; I think I was emotionally immobilized. My son cried often, my daughter too. Lucky them, and I mean that in the kindest way possible.

—Seventy-one-year-old finally-can-cry spouse

Eventually, however, if we are to live a healthy life, the mourning period needs to end, even after the loss of a child, although we may still be filled with sadness. A seventy-year-old mother shared her experience.

Losing my daughter made me realize that life does go on even after the very worst thing in life happens to you. You continue to breathe, knowing you are not the only person in the world who lost a child. You are so thankful for the almost thirty-seven years of joy she brought you, knowing many parents do not get that! You really appreciate the words "Take one day at a time" because that is the mantra that got you through the first six months. You are surprised when people make comments about your courage because you really do not have a choice. Somehow you wake up every day, put one foot before the other, realize you are still breathing. Then, one day you are again glad you are, in fact, breathing.

—Seventy-year-old finally breathing mother

—————— **MENTAL GYMNASTICS** ——————

As they aged, most of our respondents noted that they experienced the loss of some physical capabilities, which slowed them down and inhibited some activities. As the wise older person realizes, however, what really determines whether the final years of our lives are enjoyable are not our physical strengths or weaknesses but our emotional and mental ones. We may spend a lot of time walking, running, stretching, or exercising in the gym, all to help keep ourselves physically fit, but how many of us spend time exercising ourselves mentally and taking care of ourselves emotionally? Actively maintaining our emotional well-being, managing the mental scripts that affect how we feel, is critical to how well we cope when faced with the loss of a loved one and how well we adapt to aging overall. Many of our respondents recognized they needed help with this aspect of dealing with loss.

> *Some people tell me I should try to stop thinking and talking about my husband. How can I? He was part of nearly every moment of my life for nearly sixty years. I get up in the morning and his coffee cup is still there, next to mine. I'm not moving it; that's where it belongs, right next to mine.*
>
> —Ninety-two-year-old wife

One of our favorite resources for insights into increasing our emotional boundaries is *The Untethered Soul* by Michael A. Singer.[53] Singer discusses how we can keep our emotions strong and not let them control us. He suggests that we think of our thoughts as our *inner roommate* who can have a great deal of control over us. He encourages us to learn to put boundaries around that roommate, to let her or him know we will not put up with thoughts that make us feel bad or that keep us in a state of confusion, fear, sadness, or worse yet, despair. He explains the danger of getting lost in our thoughts and emotions and missing out on the fullness of life. We don't want fear to create a barrier to the outside world. Singer counsels us to remember that we have control over our emotions. We just need to remember to exercise that control.

Singer suggests experiencing the physical manifestations of our emotions: tension in our shoulders, stomach, chest, or heart. According to Singer, if we can identify the location of this emotional pain is manifested in our bodies, we can let it pass through our bodies and release the control this pain is having over us.

After a loss, fear can overtake us, but don't allow yourself to succumb to it. We can't let the fear of something bad happening to us—a stroke, a fall, or another personal loss—keep us from enjoying life to the fullest. You've probably heard that you should try to enjoy every day. As we get older, we begin to realize that we should try to enjoy every *moment*.

☞ REALITY CHECK

While it's important to prepare for loss and how best to deal with it, thinking of life in terms of one loss after another will make life not only unsatisfying but also potentially painful. This perspective drains the energy out of the precious time remaining. Another option is more positive and, we hope, more fulfilling: seeking out new experiences, relationships, and challenges. Here are some recommendations for our respondents and readers. No one will be spared loss and sadness, but we can prepare ourselves to cope. Remember:

1. Just as you can choose with whom to spend time, you can also choose your *inner roommate* (your thoughts and mental script).

2. Learn to manage and exercise your mental script in positive ways. Just as you physically train your body, train your mental script to push negative thoughts related to loss out of your mind.

3. As Singer suggests, put up a stop sign—
    literally visualize the sign—whenever your
    inner roommate wants to take your mental
    script to a depressing place.

4. Remember that staying emotionally strong is
    an active sport, not a passive one. Just as you
    can be physically fit, you become emotion-
    ally fit when you actively practice keeping
    your mental script positive. When negative
    thoughts of loss creep in, remember and visual-
    ize fun, happy times you spent with your loved
    one and replace negative thoughts with those
    positive experiences.

5. Focus on the happy years you spent with
    your loved ones, not the ones you will spend
    without them.

MOVING FORWARD

Perhaps the most important lesson we hope you learned from
this chapter is that although the death of a loved one may make
you want to withdraw and hide under the covers, you do have
options to cope with the loss. Staying connected to friends and
loved ones is key to getting past your grief. While dealing with
grief is challenging, seek out those who care for you. They may

feel awkward, not knowing what to say or do, or how to help. Help them help you by taking the initiative to stay connected.

> *Several months after a friend lost her oldest son in a motorcy-cle accident, I baked her cinnamon bread with a note saying I was thinking about her and her family. She shared how difficult it was to grieve and help her son's two young boys. She shared how the bread was a timely gift that she served at the first family meeting since the funeral. She expressed how God walked beside them every step, even by providing cinnamon bread. She helped me more than I helped her.*
> —Seventy-year-old helping-out friend

After a loss, if you continue to feel overwhelmed and depressed after what you feel is a reasonable time, consider joining a support group. Don't be afraid to speak with a grief therapist or counselor. Consider keeping a journal, even if you've never done it, to work through your feelings, especially if you've been holding your feelings in and are reluctant to share them with others.

Seek out friends and family during holidays and other special occasions that you shared with your loved one. Consider adopting new traditions that are both fun and a way to remember your friend or family member.

Moving forward after a loss doesn't mean you've forgotten about your loved one. There will be memories, lots of them. You can still cherish your memories. The goal, as we see it, is to learn to appreciate the time, whether decades, a few years, or a few months, that you spent with this special person. As writer, speaker, and Benedictine nun Joan Chittister advised, we should be filled with gratitude that we were able to share in the person's life in a meaningful way for as long as was possible.[54]

Know you have control over that mental script and actively work to keep it positive!

Chapter 10

LEARNING FROM MISTAKES AND MOVING FORWARD

"Though no one can go back in time and make
a brand-new start, anyone can start from now
and make a brand-new ending."

—Anonymous

S ome people seem to learn from their mistakes more than others, whether the lessons are in raising a family, making career decisions, or aging successfully. Those who learn from mistakes live happier, more stable lives compared to those who are unable to apply what they've learned from their own and others' experiences.

Professionals have debated why some people learn from their bad decisions and others don't. What they have determined is that those of us with healthy brains have a signal that lights up and becomes stronger when we have to make a decision that could lead us in different directions.[55] This signal alerts us that we are about to make a mistake and, hopefully, alters our course of behavior. Those capable of learning from mistakes have a healthy neurological setting that signals them at the appropriate time; thus, they struggle less with impulse control than do those with a malfunctioning signal, and they can reverse negative behaviors in the face of more and better information.

In the past, people turned to their elders for advice on how to solve a problem. There was no Google, Siri, Alexa, Wikipedia, Merriam-Webster, or Funk & Wagnalls. There were just elders who could offer help. While most of our respondents wouldn't consider themselves experts on living or aging, some of the nearly one thousand people who replied to our questionnaires, answered our interview questions, or participated in discussion groups did offer life lessons or words of wisdom based on their extensive experiences. Their comments can reassure us that our experiences and the mistakes we've made throughout our lives are more common than we may have realized. We're never too old to learn from our missteps, forgive ourselves for bad decisions in the past, and pass on to others what we've learned.

WE'RE NEVER TOO OLD
TO LEARN AND MOVE ON

Scientists tell us that our responses to our mistakes or negative actions are often a function of what we were taught about making mistakes as children. Did our parents or caregivers teach us that mistakes are something to be ashamed of or that they were simply an opportunity to learn and grow? In the best of worlds, we would have been taught that none of us are perfect, that we can learn from our mistakes, and that our parents/caregivers will still love us.

If we don't recognize or admit our mistakes, or observe the mistakes of others, we won't learn from them and we will be doomed to repeat them. If we can admit our mistakes, take responsibility for them, and change our behavior, those around us are likely to give us greater respect.

This doesn't mean that mistakes do not have consequences. Rather, our mistakes and the mistakes of others can teach us how to behave differently in the future. Mistakes are an ordinary part of life and, handled well, can imbue us with a greater sense of self-confidence and serenity.

☞ **REALITY CHECK**

You may know people who are fully aware that they

engage in negative behavior, often for extended periods of time, potentially harming themselves and others. You may even be one of these people. We hope that, even if you're resistant to changing your behavior, you'll find the following comments and suggestions helpful:

1. Popular lore says it takes anywhere from three weeks to three months to create a new habit.[56] We think it takes only three seconds to fall back into your default when confronted with a challenging situation. Your defaults are the habits or actions you resort to when a situation is difficult or stressful. They can be positive or negative. What are your defaults? Are they working for or against you? If they are working for you, great. If not, maybe it's time to change them. The first step is to be aware of what your defaults are—which ones are you satisfied with, and which ones would you like to make more effective? Maybe your default is being untruthful during highly charged, uncomfortable conversations. Or maybe you drink too much or overeat as a reaction to stress or crises. Whatever your defaults, they're strong predictors of future behavior. Once you recognize them, you can begin the process of changing them.

2. Your mistakes or the mistakes of others can help you recognize that you need to better align who you want to be with who you currently are. When you make a mistake, consider it as an opportunity to grow; this is a chance to learn from the experience and change your behavior.

3. Just as an athlete gets better through practice, you also can make fewer mistakes and less serious ones by consciously making an effort to *practice* learning from them, instead of ignoring or denying them.

4. Just because you make a mistake does not mean *you* are a mistake or a bad person.

YOU CAN NEVER UNRING A BELL

When asked the lessons they'd learned in their lifetimes, a number of respondents surprised us when they mentioned the importance of telling the truth and maintaining trust in their relationships. Some told about the guilt and shame they felt after lying, others about the pain of being lied to. In both cases, the message, as in the comments below, was that someone who lies reveals a lot about his or her character.

Always be truthful to your family, your coworkers, but especially to yourself. While it's hard for others to like you when you aren't truthful, it's even more difficult to like yourself.

—Sixty-nine-year-old liking-himself guy

Once people find out you aren't a truthful person, even if you've changed, it's hard to ever win back their trust. It's a lot easier to just be truthful right out of the box. People find out you are a lying scoundrel anyway. You are only kidding yourself if you think you can keep up a lying scam. Just ask Bill Clinton, Bernie Madoff, Richard Nixon, Anthony Weiner, John Edwards... OK, that's enough. People eventually find out the real you.

—Seventy-three-year-old knowing-it's-good-
to-be-truthful guy

☞ REALITY CHECK

It's been said that telling the truth is easier than telling a lie. Why? You don't have to keep track of different stories you've told people. The truth is one sentence. A lie is a novel. Here are some questions to contemplate when considering the importance of truthfulness in your life.

1. Have you ever been told a lie that hurt you so badly that your relationship with the person who told it was changed forever?

2. What could you have done to mend the relationship?

3. Have you ever told a lie that hurt one or more people? What were the circumstances that led to your lying? Do you regret what you did? How might you have handled the situation differently?

——— WE ALL BECOME OUR PARENTS ———

Another lesson that emerged concerned our respondents' relationships with their parents. Some recalled having little to no empathy in middle age for the physical and emotional challenges their aging parents were facing. They'd gained greater appreciation once they themselves were in their sixties, seventies, eighties, and older. Being old, they told us, had probably been more challenging for their parents than their younger selves had realized. Some noted, with sadness, that if they'd known as younger adults what they knew now about the physical and emotional challenges of aging, their relationships with their parents might have been better.

What would I do differently if I had the chance? What have I learned? I would have been more kind to my own elderly parents. I can see now how it must have been hard to be around me, because I never recognized they were growing older—or, in all honesty, I think I chose to ignore it. They were losing their hearing. They weren't moving quite as fast as they used to… It was like someone else became my parents, and I didn't like these new people. Where did my real parents go? Just when did it happen? Now that I am nearly seventy-five, I can see history repeating itself with my own kids. They are really busy. They move really fast, and they don't realize that I'm still me. So, what have I learned? That I miss those parents, those I didn't think were mine.

—Seventy-five-year-old no-longer-ignoring-it gal

Many really missed their parents and wished they would have spent more time with them. This was a common regret.

I've learned that even though I didn't like my parents very much, I really miss them now that they are gone. I wish I had worked to have a better relationship with them. It really is an odd sort of connection; even though they weren't the best parents, they were mine and I miss them.

—Eighty-two-year-old missing-his-parents guy

Others had come to learn that they'd never really known their parents and wished they'd taken time to get to know them better.

Now that [my parents] are gone, I realize I only knew them as they related to me. I didn't know them as people separate from me. This is probably why we struggled a bit. Everyone else really loved them—I mean really loved them. People told me all the time how lucky I was to have a mom and dad like mine. While I knew it to be true on some level, all I knew was how they related to me, and that was often contentious because we were always making life and day-to-day decisions. We had some fun, but I realize I didn't really know them.

—Seventy-five-year-old still-struggling gal

I would have asked my dad about being in World War II. When I think that he just left the gentle, safe confines of his home and small community one day and got on a plane to go to Europe and shoot people...I simply can't imagine it. He never spoke of it. Ever. He was such a gentle, fun-loving man. It must have been a horrendous time in his life that I never knew about or shared with him in any way. What a brave person he was forced to be. And my mom, home for a couple of years with kids, no husband, and working in a factory. I knew of things they did, but I never really knew them. I realized one day recently that other people knew my parents better than I did. I really regret that. I'd love just one day with them again. I bet I would think they were wonderful people too!

—Sixty-nine-year-old wish-she-would-have-asked gal

As the quote below suggests, some just wished they had taken more time to enjoy their families.

Beyond the obvious—to invest in Microsoft early—I think I should have just slowed down a little. If I could do it over, I would not be in such a hurry to be an adult and would have enjoyed my time with my family more. You don't realize how important they are until they are gone.

—Seventy-year-old investor guy

The man above summed up a comment we have often heard: rarely do we read on someone's tombstone "I wish I'd worked longer hours."

☞ REALITY CHECK

Adapting to the changes in those you love as they move from one developmental stage to another is difficult.

Remember how hard it was when your kids wanted more freedom as they were growing up? It was difficult to adapt. The changes your children are now witnessing in you are probably just as dramatic and difficult for them. They may occasionally show impatience, if not resentment, as a response to these changes. So what should you do? Assuming your children are astute enough to understand what you're going through, you should be open and honest with them. The following three questions might help you get started.

1. What changes are you experiencing that you could share with your children? What, if any, harm is there in doing so?

2. Are there parts of your life that your children know little or nothing about? Why do you think you're reluctant to tell them about these experiences?

3. How do you think telling them might change their understanding of who you are?

SAY IT WITH KINDNESS

We asked our respondents if there were any favorite words of wisdom or quotes they might be fond of. Their responses highlighted the importance of kindness in leading a successful, peaceful, and effective life.

Here are some of their thoughts:

I've learned that whenever I decide something with kindness, I usually make the right decision.
　　—Seventy-three-year-old making-the-right-decisions gal

I've learned that if someone says something unkind about me, I must live so that no one will believe it.
　　—Seventy-two-year-old living-in-kindness guy

I've learned that you can tell a lot about a man by the way he handles a rainy day, lost luggage, and tangled Christmas tree lights.
　　—Seventy-six-year-old handling-tough-times guy

——CHOOSE YOUR PARTNER WISELY——

Some research suggests that the divorce rate in the United States is declining, yet it remains high, with more than 40 percent of marriages ending in divorce.[57] Given the high divorce rate, we were not surprised that many of the lessons that respondents said they'd learned concerned betrayal and loss of trust in relationships. Some respondents noted that forming a new relationship after a divorce was worth the challenge of starting over, while many wished they had worked harder on their first marriages. Many realized their second marriages/relationships weren't perfect either and in some cases were much more difficult than their first. Regardless, respondents agreed that deciding whom they would marry or consider as a partner was one of the biggest decisions they ever made. None of us are perfect, and a good relationship takes work, patience, honesty, and commitment.

In several of our informal discussion groups, the topic of relationships dominated the conversation, and our respondents agreed on the importance of choosing a spouse or partner carefully. Several suggested doing some testing before committing to a relationship.

The person you choose to spend your life with is an unbelievably influential person in your life. Take your time making that choice. Be sure you know how she reacts to conflict, how she handles stress, whether she is a loyal and committed person or not, and try to really assess if this person is truthful. Can she lie easily, or is it a hard thing for her to do? It's good to "test" a bit before you commit.

—Seventy-four-year-old assessor guy

The most important decision you ever make is who you decide to marry or partner with. Choose them wisely. Don't choose them until you've gone through a difficult challenge with them, see how they manage conflict, see how they behave when they don't get their way. Everyone likes to go on vacation, enjoy the good life. We can all look like real desirable people in those situations, but our real character comes out when we have to share resources, don't get our way, or have to make difficult life decisions.

—Seventy-five-year-old choosing-carefully gal

Even in long-lasting marriages, there were some bumps along the way. Some were glad they toughed it out.

My husband and I haven't been perfect. We haven't always had the other person's interest at heart, but somehow, we never gave up on each other. We allowed each other to make mistakes, and we figured out how to forgive each other. I've learned it isn't always the big things that take down a marriage or relationship, but the day-to-day lack of thoughtfulness and unselfishness.

—Seventy-two-year-old never-gave-up gal

Others regretted sticking around.

I should have divorced my cheating husband the first time he cheated. I think I was just plain scared. Now I realize it would have been much better to have a peaceful life at age seventy-five than one where I never quite know if he's honest with me or not. Maybe my life wouldn't have been better, but I feel like I might have had more peace of mind. I could give him one mistake, but he made many. I often ask myself why I put up with him.

—Seventy-five-year-old not-so-scared-now gal

I would have learned how my wife handled disappointments in life before I would have married her.

—Sixty-five-year-old now-he-knows guy

Still others noted that sometimes their second marriages were even more challenging than the ones that had ended.

I have found my second marriage to be much more work than my first, way more work. If I had worked this hard on my first marriage, I'd still be married to her today. The problems are multiplied with her kids, my kids, and her grandkids and my grandkids. A lot of jealousy that neither of us can seem to conquer or would have ever predicted. I made a bad situation worse by divorcing my first wife.

—Seventy-three-year-old
wishes-he-worked-harder-the-first-time guy

And, finally, a few admitted the devastating blow that their unfaithfulness had on the marriage.

If I had it to do over, I would have been faithful to my wife. It's a mistake that I regret so deeply, and it's taken a lifelong toll on my wife (me too). She's forgiven me, but what a big mistake I made. I don't think I could have done anything to ever hurt her more than being unfaithful to her. Sometimes I just don't know what I was thinking.

—Seventy-one-year-old knows-he-hurt-her guy

I would not have wasted so much of my time worrying about what my husband might do. We had a tough patch a few years ago, and I spent fifteen years protecting myself from anything he might do. By this, I mean I put up emotional walls so he couldn't hurt me again. I would never let those walls down for him, but I wouldn't babysit him either. I'd continue to enjoy my life as I had always done. I'd let him figure out how to be a better person on his own. It's tough enough taking care of myself.

—Seventy-year-old stopped-worrying gal

Serious conflicts are inevitable in any close relationship, including a marriage. And when those conflicts happen, the question often arises whether to stick it out or get a divorce.

Our respondents didn't all agree on this question. On one hand, we heard that staying was a mistake and they would have been better off leaving, especially if the spouse was unfaithful. On the other hand, those who left often wondered what their lives would have been like had they been more patient, worked harder on the relationship, and stayed, even if the spouse or partner was unfaithful. On one thing they agreed: regardless of the decision, dealing with the conflict was always painful, not just for themselves but for everyone involved. The overriding message seemed to be that whatever action people take in a marriage, whether during difficult stretches or day-to-day spats, we should be kind to each other. It's easier said than done but something for all of us to work toward.

☞ REALITY CHECK

Should you stay, or should you leave? Have you wrestled with this decision? You may find it helpful to consider these questions related to your own life and spouse/partner.

1. Have you ever been tempted to leave your spouse/partner? What made you stay? Do you think you made the right decision?

2. What lessons, if any, did you learn from the experience?

3. What decisions have you made in your marriage or relationship that you regret now that you're older?

4. How might your life have turned out differently if you'd made a different decision?

LIFE IS HOW WE PERCEIVE IT

Maybe some of you know this story. Once there was a conductor on a train. At each stop, someone would ask him, "What are the people like at the next station?"

The conductor replied, "What were they like where you came from?"

The first traveler said, "They were spiteful, dishonest, and mean."

The conductor replied, "That's just how they will be at your stop."

The next passenger asked the same question. The conductor asked, "How were they where you came from?"

The passenger replied, "They were kind, always looking to help somebody in need."

The conductor replied, "They are just the same at the next stop."

The moral of the story, of course, is that our perceptions create our realities. Albert Einstein made a similar observation. One of the most important decisions we make, he said, is whether to believe the universe is friendly or hostile. The quotations below echo this message.

Reality, really, is just how you perceive it to be. Happiness is within your control. It just matters how you view each good or bad thing that happens to you.

—Sixty-nine-year-old reality kind of guy

My mom, with all of her quiet wisdom, lived a wonderful life lesson. "You've got to play the hand you're dealt," she would say. It was her clever way of telling and showing me that when something goes wrong, don't keep wishing something else had happened. Move forward and make the best of any bad situation. Don't waste precious time being unhappy about something.

She must have told my brother too—a hugely successful corporate guy. He just had a stroke, half his body doesn't work anymore, and he has yet to utter a word of complaint. He is taking each new challenge as if it were an opportunity for yet another promotion, another overseas assignment that would propel his career forward and make a better life for him and his family. I just spent two weeks with him in his rehab center. I watched with awe as he would try to get the toothpaste out of the tube with one hand; try to eat those peas on his plate with a fork in his left, not his right, hand; learn to transfer from his bed to his wheelchair with only one arm and leg, rarely showing a moment of defeat, remorse, or wishing he had another, better, different set of cards, but taking on the new challenge in his life with grace, fervor, cheerfulness, and optimism. Yes, my mom must have told him too. No doubt he was beautifully playing the hand he was dealt.

—Sixty-nine-year-old loved-her-mom's-advice gal

One respondent went so far as to say he'd learned that happiness is something you have control over.

You can choose to be happy or not. There are people who have almost nothing yet are happy, and people who have all the material things they could desire and are not happy. On the other hand, I have learned that having sufficient wealth to live the lifestyle I want to live is freeing. I also have learned that wealth is a state of mind. It is about managing your desires so that they are slightly below your income/ wealth level that keeps you happy. It doesn't matter how

much you have. If you desire more, you are not wealthy. If
you have little and desire nothing more, you are wealthy. It
is a state of mind. It is about managing your desires.

—Seventy-year-old happy guy

Many of us might want to be like the fellow quoted above, but instead, we are overwhelmed by worry about the future and endlessly replay what *could have been.* These thoughts can consume us. The danger of wasting time with worrying was another commonly repeated lesson.

I wasted too much of my life worrying (and I'm not known
as a worrying kind of person). If I've had a bad day or
hour or ten minutes, it's almost never because of something
that happened. It's because I was worrying that something
was going to happen that never did. Next time around, I
wouldn't worry about what might happen. It takes away
from enjoying today.

—Sixty-nine-year-old enjoying-today gal

CATCH THE CURVEBALLS

As young adults, many of us strived for what we thought would be a perfect life. Not only has our definition of perfect probably changed since then, but also we most likely have come to realize that living a perfect life is impossible and that *real* life constantly gets in the way of our doing so. We're thrown lots of curveballs: health problems with ourselves or loved ones, the death of a close friend or family member, career disappointments, unavoidable conflicts in our lives. How well we have adapted can make a big difference in how we face more and perhaps even greater setbacks. Here's what a few of our respondents had to say about curveballs in their lives.

Perceived or real, there simply isn't any perfect. Love the perfect imperfections of your spouse, partner, kids, and friends. Life isn't perfect. I think I used to think it could be, but now I know that is just an illusion.

—Seventy-six-year-old loving-imperfections guy

Adaptability and resilience: those are the qualities that will make you a survivor. If you think you're in control, think again. Just when you get the feeling that you've got every-thing handled and know exactly what's next, life throws you a curveball. Some people just give up then. And for them, the bend in the road is the end. But you've got to adapt to change. It's the only way to keep your head on straight and your priorities in order. I'm talking about loss, illness, and money troubles—any of the things that hit you in the gut. Nobody escapes. But the folks who get through these tough times decide to make the turn and trust in the future.

—Seventy-eight-year-old catching-the-curveballs guy

I grew up with the idea the world was black and white, good and bad, right and wrong. It took me a long time to learn that the shades of gray are where life is lived. It is managing those shades of gray with integrity that make your life both challenging and unique. Don't keep wishing it were different.

—Seventy-two-year-old living-in-the-gray-area gal

Life has a lot of gray areas. I used to think things were pretty black and white. Now I have a lot of gray. I do and say things I never thought I would do or say. I accept behavior in others and myself that I never thought I would accept. I've learned that life isn't quite so black and white as I had once thought. I'm now living in the land of "Never!"

—Seventy-year-old living-in-the-never guy

👉 REALITY CHECK

Consider these questions as you think about the personal characteristics that have helped or hindered you throughout your life.

1. What makes you happy? How has that changed since you've gotten older? What were the catalysts that brought about the change?

2. How can you use that knowledge to help you make good choices now?

3. What is your default reaction when you experience change? Resistance? Acceptance? How is that working? Do you need to consider other options?

4. What might you have done differently, given what you want now?

5. Do you think you adapt well to change?

6. What changes in your life would you make if you could make them now?

7. One helpful idea is, at the end of each day, think about what you might do differently if you could live that day over. Write down your thoughts, read them first thing in the morning, and see if this helps you make fewer mistakes the next day.

———— LEARNING FROM THE PAST ————

It's easy to fall into the trap of feeling shame or guilt about past mistakes. Sadly, there are no do-overs; however, as at other stages of life, we can be kind to ourselves and open to learning from our missteps and bad decisions. We may not be able to be a better child to our parents, but we may be able to be better parents to our adult offspring or better spouses and partners, coworkers, siblings, and friends.

It's important to never stop learning. In fact, as we get older, we may learn more about ourselves, others, and life in general.

We hope the lessons our respondents have learned are valuable, or at least entertaining, to you and help you live better in your later years. Of one thing we are sure: there are few among us who wouldn't like to have a few do-overs!

IT'S A WRAP

"Today is the oldest you've ever been and the youngest you'll ever be again."

—ELEANOR ROOSEVELT

We began this project because we wanted to understand what it means to grow older, *better*. We had a vested interest in the problem, after all, being older ourselves. Talking about aging was new territory for us, and it was new territory for everyone who graciously shared their stories with us. So, what did we learn from all our conversations? Plenty.

We learned that every older person we spoke with had the same curiosities about growing older as we did.

We learned that becoming older has taken most of us by surprise.

We learned that most of us want to figure out ways to make the rest of our years the best of our lives, as we realize that it is not every day that is valuable, but *every moment*.

We found that it was a struggle for many of us to figure out how to define ourselves and find our place in the world now that we are older.

We learned the importance of understanding our new identities as we enter the final chapter of our lives.

We learned that men and women grow more alike as they grow older.

We learned that, just as when we were young, our family members are the most important people in our lives, and the time we spend maintaining and developing those relationships is time well spent.

We learned that our circle of friends becomes smaller as we grow older, but those relationships become more valued.

We learned that we have more control over our health than we may think.

We learned that loss is one of the most difficult aspects of growing older, as we lose friends, family members, and often our own ability to care for ourselves. Yet, we learned new ways of coping when loss does occur.

We learned that most of us begin to think more intently and seriously about religion, spirituality, and faith as we grow older, and we want to find ways to use that invisible means of support to help bring solace and serenity to our lives.

We learned that we are never too old to learn from our mistakes and, while we may not be able to make a brand-new start, we can make a brand-new ending to our lives.

And finally, we learned that life is a journey, and if our journey should turn out to be a long one we will grow old. What really matters, though, is not how many years we live, but how we live those years. Each stage of our lives presents its own opportunities and challenges. While we may look back on our younger years with rose-colored glasses, if we're honest, we must admit that there were challenges to be met and problems to be solved along the way. It's the same with older age, only that the nature of the challenges and problems is different.

Getting Real about Getting Older isn't about trying to hang on to youth or pulling out all the stops to recapture some elusive, perfect moment from the past. And *Getting Real about Getting Older* isn't about growing old. It's about growing older, *better*.

Our wish for you is that this book will help you negotiate some of the more complicated aspects of your own journey. We're all on the same path, and there's comfort in knowing that others have gone before and will come after us. We wish yours to be a good journey!

Helpful Organizations and Resources

American Association of Retired Persons (AARP) provides a wealth of information on issues ranging from health to employment and finances. You can find them at www.aarp.org.

Social Security Administration can provide help with understanding Medicare requirements as well as explaining financial questions. They have local offices and can be reached via their website: www.ssa.gov.

Many older folks need help in performing their daily activities. There are all kinds of adaptive devices that make living easier—from gardening to housecleaning. Numerous companies offer these products, and a list of them is readily available online using the web search *adaptive devices for elderly*.

Alzheimer's Association—www.alz.org

American Cancer Society—www.cancer.org

American Diabetes Association—www.diabetes.org

American Heart Association—www.heart.org

Arthritis Foundation—www.arthritis.org

Medicare—www.medicare.gov

National Institutes of Health—www.nih.gov

Parkinson's Foundation—www.parkinson.org

State Resources for Seniors/Elder Care Directory Home—
    www.eldercaredirectory.org/state-resources.htm

Notes

1   P. B. Medawar, *An Unsolved Problem of Biology: An Inaugural Lecture Delivered at University College* (London: December 1961); João Pedro de Magalhães, Gerontology Information, last updated 2013, www.senescence.info/gerontology.pdf.

2   A. Weismann, *Essays Upon Heredity and Kindred Biological Problems* (Oxford: Clarendon Press, 1889).

3   J. Mitteldorf, "Aging Is Not a Process of Wear and Tear," *Rejuvenation Research* 13, no. 2–3 (2010): 322–326; A. Weismann, *Essays upon Heredity and Kindred Biological Problems.*

4   National Center for Health Statistics, Health, United States, 2016: With Chartbook on Long-term Trends in Health. Hyattsville, MD, 2017, https://www.cdc.gov/nchs/data/hus/hus16.pdf.

5   Social Security Administration, "Life Expectancy for Social Security," accessed February 15, 2018, https://www.ssa.gov/history/lifeexpect.html.

6   Gary F. Merrill, *Our Aging Bodies* (New Brunswick, NJ: Rutgers University Press, 2015); Abigail Trafford, *My Time: Making the Most of the Bonus Decades after 50* (New York: Basic Books, 2004).

7   L. E. Levine and J. Munsch, *Child Development: An Active Learning Approach* (Thousand Oaks, CA: Sage Publications, 2014); J. Lindon and K. Brodie, *Understanding Child Development 0–8 Years: Linking Theory and Practice*, 4th ed. (London: Hodder Education, 2016).

8   Jordan Gaines Lewis, "Why Does Time Fly as We Get Older?" *Scientific American*, December 18, 2013, https://blogs.scientificamerican.com/mind-guest-blog/why-does-time-fly-as-we-get-older/.

9   Tamara McClintock Greenberg, "The Invisible Years," *Psychology Today*, August 11, 2009, https://www.psychologytoday.com/blog/21st-century-aging/200908/the-invisible-years; Pamela Spahr, "Elder Invisibility: Causes, Pitfalls, and Solutions," Concordia University, Nebraska, January 13, 2015, https://online.cune.edu/elder-invisibility/; Peggy J. Kleinplatz, "Sexuality and Older People," *British Medical Journal* 337, no. 7662 (July 2008):

121–122; Kate Loveys, "The Ignored Elderly: We've Become Invisible to Society Say Half of Over 65s," *Daily Mail*, last modified May 20, 2011, http://www.dailymail.co.uk/news/article-1388922/The-ignored-elderly -Weve-invisible-society-say-half-65s.html.

10   American Patchwork & Quilting 1 Million Pillowcase Challenge, accessed February 15, 2018, http://www.allpeoplequilt.com/millionpillowcases/.

11   Cheryl Laz, "Act Your Age," *Sociological Forum* 13, no. 1 (1998): 85–113; Anil Ananthaswamy, "Why You Can't Help But Act Your Age," *Nautilus*, November 10, 2016, http://med.fsu.edu/uploads/files/Newspubs/Print /Are%20You%20as%20Old%20as%20You%20Feel_.pdf.

12   Motion Picture Association of America, *Theatrical Market Statistics 2016*, accessed February 15, 2018, http://www.mpaa.org/wp-content /uploads/2017/03/MPAA-Theatrical-Market-Statistics-2016_Final-1.pdf.

13   Ann Landers, Pfizer Get Old, accessed February 15, 2018, https://www .getold.com/oldspiration/at-age-20-we-worry-about-what-others-think-of -us-at-age-40-we-dont-care-what-they.think.

14   Kristi Pikiewicz, "Will I Still Be Me? Aging, Identity, and Self-Respect," *Psychology Today*, August 25, 2014, https://www.psychologytoday.com/blog /meaningful-you/201408/will-i-still-be-me-aging-identity-and-self-respect.

15   Joel R. Sneed and Susan Krauss Whitbourne, "Identity Processing and Self-Consciousness in Middle and Later Adulthood," *Journals of Gerontology, Series B, Psychological Sciences and Social Sciences* 58, no. 6 (2003): 313–319.

16   Linda P. Fried, "Making Aging Positive," *The Atlantic*, June 1, 2014, https ://www.theatlantic.com/health/archive/2014/06/valuing-the-elderly -improving-public-health/371245/.

17   "Health, United States, 2016."

18   Samantha Olson, "Aging Differences Between Men And Women: How The Sexes Grow Old Together (And Apart)," Medical Daily, January 21, 2015, http://www.medicaldaily.com/aging-differences-between-men-and -women-how-sexes-grow-old-together-and-apart-318632.

19   Diana Howard, "Is a Man's Skin Really Different?" The International Dermal Institute, 2017, accessed March 16, 2018, https://www.dermalinstitute .com/us/library/17_article_Is_a_Man_s_Skin_Really_Different_.html.

20   N. Raz, "The Aging Brain: Structural Changes and Their Implications for Cognitive Aging," in *New Frontiers in Cognitive Aging*, eds. R. Dixon, L.

Bäckman, and L. Nilsson (New York Oxford University Press, 2004), 115–134.

21   Raz, "The Aging Brain."

22   Roy F. Baumeister, "The Reality of the Male Sex Drive," *Psychology Today*, December 8, 2010, https://www.psychologytoday.com/blog /cultural-animal/201012/the-reality-the-male-sex-drive.

23   Michael Gurian, *The Wonders of Aging: A New Approach to Embracing Life After Fifty* (New York: Atria, 2013).

24   Mandy Oaklander, "Old People Are Happier Than People in Their 20s," *Time* magazine, August 24, 2016, http://time.com/4464811 /aging-happiness-stress-anxiety-depression/.

25   Irving Weiner, "Social Relationships in the Content of Health," in *Developmental Psychology*, vol. 6, eds. T. Millon et al., in *Handbook of Psychology*, ed. I. Weiner (Hoboken, NJ: John Wiley & Sons, 2003), 493.

26   E. H. Erikson, *Childhood and Society* (New York: Norton, 1950).

27   N. Marks, J. D. Lambert, and H. Choi, "Transitions to Caregiving, Gender, and Psychological Well-Being: A Prospective U.S. National Study," *Journal of Marriage and Family* 64, (2002): 657–667; M. Pinquart and S. Sorensen, "Differences between Caregivers and Noncaregivers in Psychological Health and Physical Health: A Meta-Analysis," *Psychology and Aging* 18, no. 2 (2003): 250–267.

28   Michele Salomon et al., *Stress in America: Our Health at Risk*, American Psychological Association, January 11, 2012, https://www.apa.org/news /press/releases/stress/2011/final-2011.pdf.

29   J. Panula et al., "Mortality and Cause of Death in Hip Fracture Patients Aged 65 or Older: A Population-Based Study," *BMC Musculoskeletal Disorders* 12 (May 2011): 105, doi: 10.1186/1471-2474-12-105.

30   "Have You Ever Been Lonely?" music by Peter De Rose, lyrics by Billy Hill, 1932.

31   "Depression: What You Need to Know," National Institute of Mental Health, accessed February 15, 2018, https://www.nimh.nih.gov/health /publications/depression-what-you-need-to-know/index.shtml.

32   Karen K. Brees, *The Everything Health Guide to Depression: Reassuring*

Advice to Help You Feel Like Yourself Again (Avon, MA: Adams Media F+W Publications, 2008).

33   Karina W. Davidson, "Depression and Coronary Heart Disease," *ISRN Cardiology* 2012 (2012): doi:10.5402/2012/743813.

34   Mary Jo Kreitzer, "Why Personal Relationships Are Important," Taking Charge of Your Health and Wellbeing, University of Minnesota, accessed March 16, 2018, https://www.takingcharge.csh.umn.edu /why-personal-relationships-are-important.

35   Linda K. Stroh, *Trust Rules: How to Tell the Good Guys from the Bad Guys in Work and Life* (Santa Barbara, CA: Praeger, 2015).

36   S. T. Charles and J. R. Piazza, "Memories of Social Interactions: Age Differences in Emotional Intensity," *Psychology and Aging* 22 (2007): 300–309; Gloria Luong, Susan T. Charles, and Karen L. Fingerman, "Better with Age: Social Relationships Across Adulthood," *Journal of Social and Personal Relationships* 28, no. 1 (February 2011): 9–23.

37   Susan Krauss Whitbourne, "What Rising Divorce Rates in Midlife Mean for You," *Psychology Today*, November 9, 2013, https://www.psychologytoday .com/blog/fulfillment-any-age/201311/what-rising-divorce-rates-in-midlife -mean-you; S. L. Brown and I. F. Lin, "The Gray Divorce Revolution: Rising Divorce Among Middle-Aged and Older Adults, 1990–2010," *Journals of Gerontology, Series B, Psychological Sciences and Social Sciences* 67B (2012): 731–741.

38   Brown and Lin, "The Gray Divorce Revolution."

39   Jeffrey L. Greif and Michael E. Woolley, *Adult Sibling Relationships* (New York: Columbia University Press, 2015).

40   Alix Spiegel, "Big Sibling's Big Influence: Some Behaviors Run In The Family," *All Things Considered*, NPR, April 29, 2013, https://www .npr.org/sections/health-shots/2013/04/29/179266284/Big-Siblings -Big-Influence-Some-Behaviors-Run-In-The-Family.

41   Spiegel, "Big Sibling's Big Influence."

42   Greif and Woolley, *Adult Sibling Relationships*.

43   Barbara Graham, *Eye of My Heart* (New York: Harper Collins Publishing, 2010).

44   Vikki Claflin, "14 Contrasts between Parenting and Grandparenting,"

Scary Mommy, accessed February 15, 2018, www.scarymommy.com /parenting-and-grandparenting/.

45   Terri Orbuch, "Avoid the Grandparent Trap: Six Ways to Build Stronger Bonds That Last a Lifetime," Next Avenue, February 3, 2012, www .nextavenue.org/avoid-grandparent-trap.

46   Nancy P. Kropf and Susan Kelley, "Why More Grandparents Are Raising Their Grandchildren," The Conversation, September 8, 2017, https://phys .org/news/2017-09-grandparents-grandchildren.html.

47   Graham, *Eye of My Heart.*

48   R. S. Porter, et al, *The Merck Manual of Diagnosis and Therapy* (Whitehouse Station, NJ: Merck Sharp & Dohme Corp., 2011).

49   Harold G. Koenig, "Religion, Spirituality, and Health: The Research and Clinical Implications," *ISRN Psychiatry* 2012 (2012): doi:10.5402/2012/278730.

50   Judith Viorst, *Necessary Losses* (New York: Free Press, 1998), 17.

51   E. Kübler-Ross, *On Grief and Grieving: Finding the Meaning of Grief Through the Five Stages of Loss* (New York: Simon & Schuster, 2005).

52   Teddi D. Johnson, "Healthy Relationships Lead to Better Lives," *The Nation: A Publication of the American Public Health Association* 46 (August 2017): 6.

53   Michael A. Singer, *The Untethered Soul: The Journey Beyond Yourself* (Oakland, CA: New Harbinger Publications, 2007).

54   Joan Chittister, *The Gift of Years: Growing Older Gracefully* (Katonah, NY: Bluebridge, 2008).

55   Nayanah Siva, "Why We Don't Learn from Our Mistakes," Center for Memory and Brain (Boston: Boston University Press, 2012).

56   Maria Popova, "How Long It Takes to Form a New Habit," Brain Pickings, accessed February 15, 2018, https://www.brainpickings.org/2014/01/02 /how-long-it-takes-to-form-a-new-habit.

57   Abigail Abrams, "Divorce Rate in U.S. Drops to Nearly 40-Year Low," *Time* magazine, last modified December 5, 2016, http://time.com/4575495 /divorce-rate-nearly-40-year-low/.

Bibliography

Brees, Karen K. *The Everything Health Guide to Depression: Reassuring Advice to Help You Feel Like Yourself Again*. Avon, MA: Adams Media F+W Publications, 2008.

————. *Blue Zones: Lessons for Living Longer From the People Who've Lived the Longest*. Washington, DC: National Geographic, 2008.

Buettner, Dan. *Thrive: Finding Happiness the Blue Zones Way*. Washington, DC: National Geographic, 2011.

Charles, S. T. and J. R. Piazza. "Memories of Social Interactions: Age Differences in Emotional Intensity." *Psychology and Aging* 22 (2007): 300–309.

Chittister, Joan. *The Gift of Years*. Katonah. New York: Blue Bridge, 2010.

Crowley, Chris and Henry S. Lodge. *Younger Next Year*. New York: Workman Publishing, 2005.

Dalai Lama and Desmond Tutu. *The Book of Joy*. New York: Random House, 2016.

Gawande, Atul. *Being Mortal*. London: Profile Books LTD, 2015.

Gray, John. *Men Are from Mars, Women Are from Venus: The*

Classic Guide to Understanding the Opposite Sex. New York: HarperCollins Publishers, 2012.

Hammond, Claudia. *Time Warped: Unlocking the Mysteries of Time Perception*. New York: HarperCollins Publishers, 2013.

Luong, G., S. T. Charles, and K. L. Fingerman. "Better with Age: Social Relationships Across Adulthood." *Journal of Social and Personal Relationships* 1, no. 28 (2011): 9–23.

McCoy, Kathy. *We Don't Talk Anymore: Healing after Parents and Their Adult Children Become Estranged*. Naperville, IL: Sourcebooks, 2017.

Nevins, Sheila. *You Don't Look Your Age...and Other Fairy Tales*. New York: Flatiron Books, 2017.

O'Toole, James. *Creating the Good Life*. New York: Rodale, 2005.

Pillemer, Karl. *30 Lessons for Living*. New York: Penguin Group, 2011.

Porter, R. S., J. L. Kaplan, and Merck & Co. *The Merck Manual of Diagnosis and Therapy*. Whitehouse Station, NJ: Merck Sharp & Dohme Corp., 2011.

Rankin, Lissa. *Mind Over Medicine*. New York: Hay House, Inc., 2013.

Rosenblatt, Roger. *Rules for Aging*. New York: Harcourt, Inc., 2000.

Sacks, Oliver. *Gratitude*. New York: Alfred A. Knopf, 2016.

Sandberg, Sheryl and Adam Grant. *Option B*. New York: Alfred A. Knopf, 2017.

Sellers, Ronnie. *70 Things to Do When You Turn 70.* South Portland: Sellers Publishing, 2013.

Singer, Michael, A. *The Untethered Soul: The Journey Beyond Yourself.* Oakland, CA: New Harbinger Publications, 2007.

Stovall, Jim. *The Ultimate Gift.* Colorado Springs: David C. Cook, 2001.

Stroh, Linda. K. *Trust Rules: How to Tell the Good Guys from the Bad Guys in Work and Life.* Santa Barbara, CA: Praeger Publishing, 2015.

Thaler, Linda Kaplan and Robin Kovel. *The Power of Nice.* New York: Doubleday, 2006.

Ukleja, Mick and Robert Lorber. *Who Are You and What Do You Want?* Des Moines: Meredith Books, 2008.

Vaillant, George, E. *Aging Well.* New York: Little Brown & Co., 2002.

Viorst, Judith. *I'm Too Young to Be Seventy.* New York: The Free Press, 2005.

———. *Necessary Losses.* New York: The Free Press, 1986.

Weil, Andrew. *Healthy Aging.* New York: Anchor Books, 2005.

Index

D

E

P

S

Acknowledgments

We'd like to thank Anna Michels, our editor at Sourcebooks, for believing in our project and for being so enjoyable to work with. We'd especially like to thank everyone who responded to our questionnaire, those who participated in our interviews and discussion groups, and those with whom we spent long hours discussing how to grow older, *better*. Thanks also to Angie Gittleman, Brad Stroh, Erica Fox, and others who offered edits and advice on our manuscript. Their contributions are the heart and soul of our book.

About the Authors

Linda K. Stroh is an award-winning professor emerita of organizational behavior and human development at Loyola University Chicago who now teaches at the University of California, Santa Cruz. Linda received her PhD in human development at Northwestern University and earned a postdoctorate in organizational behavior from Northwestern University's Kellogg Graduate School of Management. Her books and research have been featured in the *Wall Street Journal*, the *New York Times*, the *Washington Post*, *Oprah & Friends Radio*, CNBC, and *NBC Nightly News*, among other national and international publications. Linda has been frequently consulted as an expert for various news and popular press outlets. Her most recent book, *Trust Rules: How to Tell the Good Guys from the Bad Guys in Work and Life*, was recommended by *US News & World Report* for all executives' nightstands.

Linda has served on the boards of directors of the Excelligence Corporation, the Center for Employment Dispute Resolution, the Human Resource Management Association of Chicago, and Big Brothers Big Sisters of Lake County. She also served for many years as the academic advisor to the International Personnel Association, an association of thirty of the top multinational companies in the United States and Canada.

Linda is most proud, however, to be a wife, mother, grandmother, sister, and friend to the most important people in her life.

Photo by John Brees

Karen K. Brees has worked in a bakery, been a bookmobile librarian, an office manager, a classroom teacher, and a university professor. After retiring from teaching, she took the advice of *Getting Real about Getting Older*, and kept growing and taking on new challenges. She's currently an academic editor and writer and the author or coauthor of six books in the medical and general interest fields. Writing as Karen K. Brees, PhD, her titles include *The Everything Health Guide to Depression, The Complete Idiot's Guide to Arthritis,* and *The Complete Idiot's*

Guide to Preserving Food. She is also the award-winning author of two novels, *Headwind: The Intrepid Adventures of OSS Agent Katrin Nissen* and *The Esposito Caper*. Learn more about Brees by visiting her website at karenkbrees.com.